Media Law in Slovenia

Media Law in Slovenia

Second Edition

Rado Bohinc

This book was originally published as a monograph in the International Encyclopaedia of Laws/Media Law.

Founding Editor: Roger Blanpain
General Editor: Frank Hendrickx
Volume Editors: Peggy Valcke & Eva Lievens

Wolters Kluwer

Published by:
Kluwer Law International B.V.
PO Box 316
2400 AH Alphen aan den Rijn
The Netherlands
E-mail: international-sales@wolterskluwer.com
Website: lrus.wolterskluwer.com

Sold and distributed in North, Central and South America by:
Wolters Kluwer Legal & Regulatory U.S.
7201 McKinney Circle
Frederick, MD 21704
United States of America
Email: customer.service@wolterskluwer.com

Sold and distributed in all other countries by:
Air Business Subscriptions
Rockwood House
Haywards Heath
West Sussex
RH16 3DH
United Kingdom
Email: international-customerservice@wolterskluwer.com

Printed on acid-free paper

ISBN 978-94-035-1773-5

e-Book: ISBN 978-94-035-1790-2
web-PDF: ISBN 978-94-035-1834-3

Printed in the United Kingdom.

The Author

Rado Bohinc (b. 1949) graduated from the University of Ljubljana, Faculty of Law (1971). He received a Master of Laws (Ljubljana, 1985) and Doctor of Law (Ljubljana, 1987). His doctoral thesis was on the relationship between property rights and corporate governance. He was appointed assistant professor at the University of Ljubljana, Faculty of Social Sciences in 1986, and has been teaching company, securities, labour and European Union (EU) law since then. He served as a Minister of Science and Technology (1992–1996) and as Minister of Internal Affairs (2000–2004) in the Slovene government. In 1999, he was a Fulbright scholar at the University of California School of Law. In 2003, he was appointed a full-time professor at the University of Ljubljana and the University of Maribor. He was President of the Council of the Slovene Science Foundation. In November 2007, he was elected rector of the University of Primorska, Slovenia. Since November 2011 he is again a full-time professor of corporate, securities and EU law at University of Ljubljana, Faculty of Social Sciences. He is author of several articles and books on company and securities law, labour law and EU law. He is one of the authors of the Commentary on the Slovene Law on Commercial Companies, edited in 2007. He has written several books on company law, labour and public servants' law, corporate governance, public law entities, and other subjects. Some of his books are: *Social Responsibility*, Ljubljana: Založba FDV, 2017 (Slovene), *Corporations and Partnerships in Slovenia*, Alphen an den Rijn: Kluwer Law International, cop. 2014; *Comparative Company Law (An Overview on US and some EU Countries' Corporate Governance Legislation*, dr. Miller: VDM Verlag, 2011) and in *Slovene: Corporations* (2011); *Law of the EU* (2007); *Public Law Entities* (2005), *Corporate Governance* (co-author B. Bratina) (2005); *Labour and Public Servant Relations* (2003); *Corporate Governance in the US, EU and Slovenia – A Comparative Analysis* (2000); *The Director of the Business Corporation* (co-author I. Ivanjko) (1999).

The Author

Table of Contents

Table of Contents

List of Abbreviations

AJPES	Agency of the Republic of Slovenia for Public Legal Records and Related Services
AKOS (APEK)	Communications Networks and Services Agency
H^	
APIA	Access to Public Information Act
ARTV	Act on Radio and Television Corporation of Slovenia
AVMS	Audio-visual Media Services
AVMSA	Act on Audio-Visual Media Services
CAS	Conditional Access Systems
CATV	Cable Television
CO	Code of Obligations
DBA	Digital Broadcasting Act
DVB-T	Digital Video Broadcasting-Terrestrial (TV)
ECA	Electronic Communications Act
ECC	Electronic Communications Council
ECESA	The Electronic Commerce and Electronic Signature Act
EU	European Union
IP	Intellectual Property
IT	Information Technology
MMA	Mass Media Act
PC	Penal Code
PDPA	Personal Data Protection Act
SPAA	Slovenian Press Agency Act
TV	Television

List of Abbreviations

General Introduction

§1. General Background of the Country

I. Political and Legal System of the Country

A. *Introduction*

1. At various points in Slovenia's history, the country has been part of the Roman Empire; the Duchy of Carantania; Austria-Hungary; the State of Slovenes, Croats and Serbs; the Kingdom of Serbs, Croats and Slovenes (renamed the Kingdom of Yugoslavia in 1929) between the World Wars; and the Socialist Federal Republic (SFR) of Yugoslavia from 1945 until gaining independence in 1991.

B. *State Structure*

2. According to its Constitution,[1] Slovenia is a democratic republic, a State governed by the rule of law and a social State. The Slovenian head of State is the President, who is elected by popular vote every five years. The executive branch is headed by the prime minister and the council of ministers or cabinet, which are elected by the Parliament.

3. The bicameral Parliament of Slovenia consists of the National Assembly (Državni zbor), and the National Council (Državni svet). The National Assembly has ninety seats, which are partially filled with directly elected representatives, and partially with proportionally elected representatives (two seats reserved for autochthonous Hungarian and Italian minorities).

4. The National Council has forty seats, and is made up of representatives of social, economic, professional and local interest groups. Parliamentary elections are held every four years.

5. Slovenia is a member of the European Union (EU), the Council of Europe and North Atlantic Treaty Organization (NATO).Slovenia is also a founding member of

1. The Constitution of the Republic of Slovenia (CRS) was adopted on 23 Dec. 1991, and amended on 14 Jul. 1997, 25 Jul. 2000 and 7 Mar. 2003, URS.

the World Trade Organization, joined Central European Free Trade Agreement (CEFTA) in 1996, and joined the EU on 1 May 2004.

C. Division of Competences Between the State and the Community Level

6. Slovenia's statistical regions exist solely for legal and statistical purposes. The government, however, is preparing a plan for new administrative regions. The number of these regions has not yet been decided, but is said to be between twelve and fourteen. Constitutional changes allowing the creation of regions have already been approved by the National Assembly.

7. Slovenia is divided into 210 municipalities, of which eleven have urban status.

D. Geography, Population, Life Standard and Economy

1. Geography

8. The Republic of Slovenia (Republika Slovenija) lies in southern Central Europe bordering Italy on the west, the Adriatic Sea on the southwest, Croatia on the south and east, Hungary on the northeast, and Austria on the north.

9. The capital of Slovenia is Ljubljana. Four major European geographic regions meet in Slovenia: the Alps, the Dinarides, the Pannonian plain, and the Mediterranean. Slovenia's highest peak is Triglav (2,864 m); the country's average height above sea level is 557 m.

2. Population

10. On 1 April 2018, Slovenia had a population of 2,067,284. The number of Slovene citizens decreased while the number of foreign citizens increased and reached 6.0%.

	1. April 2017	*1. July 2017*	*1. October 2017*	*1. January 2018*	*1. April 2018*
Population	*2,064,836*	*2,066,161*	*2,065,890*	*2,066,880*	*2,067,284*
Men	1,025,013	1,025,973	1,026,100	1,027,041	1,028,014
Women	1,039,823	1,040,188	1,039,790	1,039,839	1,039,270
Citizens of the Republic of Slovenia	1,948,995	1,948,525	1,946,257	1,945,005	1,943,441

	1. April 2017	*1. July 2017*	*1. October 2017*	*1. January 2018*	*1. April 2018*
Men	949,791	949,644	948,652	948,185	947,657
Women	999,204	998,881	997,605	996,820	995,784
Foreign citizens	115,841	117,636	119,633	121,875	123,843
Men	75,222	76,329	77,448	78,856	80,357
Women	40,619	41,307	42,185	43,019	43,486

Source: SURS.

The population of Slovenia has been *increasing only due to immigration*, while the birth rate has been negative since 1993. The age structure is changing not only because of the decreased birth rate but also due to longer life. Like in other developed countries, Slovenia's population is ageing. The literacy rate is 99.7% of the total population.

11. Approximately *one-third of the population live in towns* with more than 10,000 inhabitants, the rest live in nearly six thousand smaller towns and villages.[2]

Among the working population in Slovenia, 14.6% of people were born abroad. Of these, half were born in Bosnia and Herzegovina, while the majority of the people were born in Croatia (slightly less than 18% of the economically active foreign born).

12. Among the *working population*, born in Slovenia, most have secondary education (almost 60% of people), as well as the workforce born abroad, is dominated by persons with secondary education, but their proportion is lower (almost 48%). Of the people born in Slovenia, majority are tertiary educated (almost 26%), whereas those born abroad, are primary-educated or less (41%).[3]

13. In Slovenia, the *main ethnic groups* comprises Slovenians (84%). Nationalities from the former Yugoslavia (Serbs, Croats, Bosniaks and Muslims by nationality) form 6.3% and the Hungarian, Italian and Roma minorities form 0.6% of the population. The ethnic affiliation of 9.1% is either undeclared or unknown.

14. Population *density* in Slovenia is about a hundred inhabitants per km^2 (256/sq. mi), which is much lower than in the majority of European States (compared with 320/km^2 for the Netherlands or 195/km^2 for Italy). Approximately 51% of the population lives in urban areas and 49% in rural areas.

2. Slovenia.si: http://www.slovenia.si/slovenia/country/people/population/.
3. Socioeconomic characteristics of the population (1 Jan. 2009) and international migrants (2009), detailed data, Slovenia – final data.

3. Employment

15. In terms of employment, 66% of people aged 15-64 in Slovenia have a paid job, slightly below the 67% OECD employment average.[4]

In 2017, the ILO *unemployment rate was 6.6%* (the lowest in the past eight years), 1.4 percentage points lower than in 2016. The number of employed persons (959,000) increased by 4.8%, while the number of unemployed persons (67,000) decreased by 15.4% compared to 2016 (SURS).

16. The number of *employees* has been increasing. In 2017, there were 819,000 employees: 4.3% (34,000) more than in 2016 and 9.7% (73,000) more than in 2014. Most of them were employees in labour relation. Among those, 672,000 employees were permanently employed (3.4% more than in 2016), 101,000 were temporarily employed (7.8% more than in 2016), followed by student workers (33,000 or 7.6% more than in 2016) and employees in other forms of work (13,000).

4. Life Standard

17. Slovenia performs well in some measures of well-being in the *Better Life Index (2018)*. Slovenia ranks above the average in housing, health status, social connections, education and skills, work-life balance, environmental quality, and personal security. It is below average in income and wealth, job and earnings, civic engagement, and subjective well-being.[5]

In Slovenia, *87% of adults aged 25–64 have completed upper secondary education*, higher than the OECD average of 74%. This is truer of men than women, as *89% of men* have successfully completed high school compared with 86% of women.

In Slovenia, *the average household net-adjusted disposable income per capita is USD 20,505 a year*, which is lower than the OECD average of USD 30,563 a year. There is a *considerable gap between the rich and poor* – the top 20% of the population earn close to four times as much as the bottom 20%.

18. In terms of employment, *66% of people aged 15-64 in Slovenia in 2018 have a paid job*, slightly below the 67% OECD employment average. Some 69% of men are in paid work, compared with 63% of women. In Slovenia, *87% of adults aged 25–64 have completed upper secondary education*, higher than the OECD average of 74%.

19. In terms of health, *life expectancy in Slovenia is 81 years*, one year higher than the OECD average in 2018. Life expectancy for women is 84 years, compared with 78 for men. About *89% of people say they are satisfied with the quality of the water*, considerably higher than the OECD average of 81%.

---

4. OECD Better Life Index http://www.oecdbetterlifeindex.org/countries/slovenia/.
5. Data are taken from OECD Better Life Index 2018, http://www.oecdbetterlifeindex.org/countries/slovenia/.

20. Concerning the public sphere, in 2018, there was a strong sense of community and a moderate level of civic participation in Slovenia, where *91% of people believed that they knew someone they could rely on in time of need*, broadly in line with the OECD average of 89%.

5. Economy

21. Macroeconomic and financial stability[6] have allowed Slovenia to complete the process of European integration by joining the euro area on 1 January 2007. Slovenia was the first new member to adopt the euro as the country's only currency on 1 January 2007. In June 2004, it joined the European Exchange Rate Mechanism.

Economic growth in Slovenia in 2017 was significantly higher than in the previous years and among the highest in the euro area. GDP growth stood at 5.0% in 2017, and was particularly high in the final quarter (6.0%), the second-highest rate in the euro area. The growth was broadly based and founded on *the* growth in household consumption (3.2%), significant growth in gross investment (8.4%), and strengthening growth in the exports of merchandise and services (10.6%). Economic growth remained relatively high in the first quarter of 2018. *The ratio of investment to GDP increased slightly, while there was a pronounced increase in saving in the wake of the favourable situation on the labour market.*[7]

According to OECD 2017 Economic Survey, *growth* has picked up to a pace *exceeding the EU15* average, thanks to recent structural reforms, business restructuring, supportive monetary conditions and improved export markets. *Lower unemployment* and higher real incomes are underpinning consumption. *Business investment is rising*, although it remains low relative to GDP. *Public debt and non-performing loans are being reduced* from high levels. However, Slovenia faces several socioeconomic challenges, particularly rapid population ageing. The government's National Development Strategy 2030 aims to improve the well-being of its people through strong, inclusive and sustainable growth in the context of the United Nations' Sustainable Development Goals.[8]

22. Slovenia's trade is oriented towards Western (EU) countries, mainly Germany, Austria, Italy and France. This is the result of a wholesale reorientation of trade towards the West and the growing markets of Central and Eastern Europe in the wake of the collapse of its Yugoslav markets. Slovenia's economy is highly dependent on foreign trade.

23. Trade equals about 120% of GDP (exports and imports combined). About two-thirds of Slovenia's trade is with EU members, a primary motivation for seeking EU membership.

---

6. Bank of Slovenia, Financial Stability Review, Expert Papers on Financial Stability 2006, www.bsi.si/ en/default.asp.
7. Bank of Slovenia, Euro system, Financial Stability Review, 2018.
8. OECD Economic Surveys Slovenia, September 2017, Overview: http://www.oecd.org/eco/surveys/Slovenia-2017-OECD-economic-survey-overview.pdf.

24. Industry and construction comprise over one-third of the GDP. As in most industrial economies, services make up an increasing share of output (57.1%), notably in financial services.

II. Social and Cultural Values

A. Language, Religion, Culture

25. The official language is Slovenian, which is a member of the South Slavic language group. Hungarian and Italian enjoy the status of official languages in the ethnically mixed regions along the Hungarian and Italian borders.

26. By religion, Slovenians have traditionally been largely Roman Catholic.

27. Slovenia's first book was printed by the Protestant reformer Primož Trubar (1508–1586). Mainly two books, Catechismus (a catechism) and Abecedarium, were published in 1550 in Tübingen, Germany.

28. Slovenia's two greatest writers were the poet France Prešeren (1800–1849) and the writer Ivan Cankar (1876–1918). The most important Slovenian painters are Ivana Kobilca and impressionist Rihard Jakopič. The most famed Slovenian architect is Joee Plečnik, who worked in Vienna as well as in Prague.

B. Education System

29. The Slovenian educational system consists of *pre-school* education, basic education – there is one structure for primary and lower *secondary* education – and (upper) secondary education, which includes vocational and technical education, secondary general education, higher vocational education and higher education. Specific parts of the system are adult education, music and dance education, special needs education and programmes in ethnically and linguistically mixed areas.

30. Currently there are four *universities* in Slovenia: University of Ljubljana, University of Maribor, University of Primorska and University of Nova Gorica.

C. Social, Cultural and Human Values

31. According to its Constitution, Slovenia, in its own territory, protects *human rights and fundamental freedoms.*

32. It is a Constitutional obligation to provide for the preservation of the natural wealth and cultural *heritage* and create opportunities for the harmonious development of society and culture in Slovenia.

33. The right to *social security* is a Constitutional right. Citizens have the right to social security under conditions provided by law. The State regulates compulsory health, pensions, disability and other social insurance, and ensures its proper functioning. The right to *health* care is also a Constitutional right, as follows: Everyone has the right to health care under conditions provided by law. By law, cost of health care must be provided from public funds.

34. Freedom of *education* is constitutionally guaranteed. Primary education is compulsory and is financed from public funds. The State creates the opportunities for citizens to obtain a proper education. State universities and institutions of higher education are autonomous. The freedom of scientific and artistic endeavour is constitutionally guaranteed.

III. Overview of the Slovenian Constitutional Situation in the Context of Broadcasting and Telecommunications Regulation

A. General on Rights and Freedoms in the Constitution of Slovenia

35. Freedoms and rights of major direct relevance for the media law in Slovenia are the *freedom of expression* and the *right to correction and reply*. But there are other fundamental rights that form the Constitutional framework for democratic and opened society; for example here are some of them:

- *Equality before the Law* (Article 14 of the Constitution of Slovenia, hereinafter CS); in Slovenia everyone shall be guaranteed equal human rights and fundamental freedoms irrespective of national origin, race, sex, language, religion, political or other conviction, material standing, birth, education, social status, disability or any other personal circumstance. All are equal before the law.
- *Protection of Human Personality and Dignity* (Article 21 of the CS); respect for human personality and dignity is guaranteed in criminal and in all other legal proceedings, as well as during the deprivation of liberty and enforcement of punitive sanctions.
- *Equal Protection of Rights* (Article 22 of the CS); everyone is guaranteed equal protection of rights in any proceeding before a court and before other state authorities, local community authorities and bearers of public authority that decide on his rights, duties or legal interests.
- *Public Nature of Court Proceedings* (Article 24 of the CS); court hearings are public. Judgments are pronounced publicly.
- *Presumption of Innocence (*Article 27 of the CS); any person charged with a criminal offence is presumed innocent until found guilty in a final judgment.
- *Right to Personal Dignity and Safety* (Article 34 of the CS); everyone has the right to personal dignity and safety.
- *Protection of Right to Privacy and Personality Rights* (Article 35 of the CS); the inviolability of the physical and mental integrity of every person, his privacy and personality rights is guaranteed.

- *Protection of the Privacy of Correspondence and Other Means of Communication* (Article 37 of the CS); the privacy of correspondence and other means of communication is guaranteed.
- *Protection of Personal Data (*Article 38 of the CS)*;* the protection of personal data is guaranteed. The use of personal data contrary to the purpose for which it was collected is prohibited. The collection, processing, designated use, supervision and protection of the confidentiality of personal data is provided by law.
- *Freedom of Conscience (*Article 41 of the CS); religious and other beliefs may be freely professed in private and public life.
- *Participation in the Management of Public Affairs* (Article 44 of the CS); every citizen has the right, in accordance with the law, to participate either directly or through elected representatives in the management of public affairs.
- *Prohibition of Incitement to Discrimination and Intolerance and Prohibition of Incitement to Violence and War* (Article 63); any incitement to national, racial, religious or other discrimination, and the inflaming of national, racial, religious or other hatred and intolerance are unconstitutional. Any incitement to violence and war is unconstitutional.

B. Freedom of Expression

36. Article 39 of the Constitution of Slovenia stipulates freedom of expression as one of the *fundamental Constitutional freedoms*. Freedom of expression encompasses freedom of thought, freedom of speech and freedom of public appearance. Freedom of expression further on includes freedom of the press and other forms of public communication and expression. According to the Constitution of Slovenia freedom of expression shall be guaranteed.

37. Constitution of Slovenia guarantees everyone to freely *collect, receive and disseminate* information and opinions. Except in such cases as are provided by law, everyone has the right to obtain information of a public nature in which he/she has a well-founded legal interest under law (Article 39 of the Constitution of Slovenia).

C. Right to Correction and Reply

38. The right to correct published information which has damaged a right or interest of an individual, organization or body is guaranteed, as it is the right to reply to such published information (Article 40 of the Constitution of Slovenia).Both rights (Correction and Reply) are in details elaborated in the respective Law on Mass Media.

D. Exercise, Limitation and Temporary Suspension of Rights and Fundamental Freedoms

39. According to Article 15 of the Constitution of Slovenia, human rights and fundamental freedoms are *exercised directly on the basis of the Constitution*. The manner in which human rights and fundamental freedoms are exercised may be regulated by law whenever the Constitution so provides or where this is necessary due to the particular nature of an individual right or freedom.

40. Human rights and fundamental freedoms could only be limited only by the rights of others and in such cases as are provided by the Constitution. Judicial protection of human rights and fundamental freedoms, and the right to obtain redress for the violation of such rights and freedoms, is guaranteed by the Constitution.

41. According to Article 16 of the Constitution of Slovenia, some of the human rights and fundamental freedoms provided by the Constitution may exceptionally be *temporarily suspended or restricted* during a war and state of emergency, but only to the extent required by such circumstances and inasmuch as the measures adopted do not create inequality based solely on race, national origin, sex, language, religion, political or other conviction, material standing, birth, education, social status or any other personal circumstance.

42. For some rights, Constitution of Slovenia does *not allow any temporary suspension* or restriction (for example: Inviolability of Human Life, Prohibition of Torture, Protection of Human Personality and Dignity, Presumption of Innocence, Principle of Legality in Criminal Law, Legal Guarantees in Criminal Proceedings and Freedom of Conscience).

§2. The Media Landscape

I. Overview of Media Markets and Main Actors

A. Introduction

1. Summary

43. There is *no comprehensive analysis* of Slovenian media landscape; there is still no government strategy (it is foreseen) in the media field, which would respond to the issues of media space, both public and private, and outlined at least medium-term guidelines.

National Programme for Culture 2014–2017 envisages adopting a *separate media strategy* for 2015–2020; measures and actions should be proposed to *increase the readership* of good general-interest newspapers and magazines providing information and to *boost the quality and volume of media* content in areas such as culture and arts, education and training, health, science, protection of the environment, etc. In the context of rapid development of this field, *the role and scope of the public radio and television network will be examined*; outstanding radio and television programmes that are in the public interest should be given *additional support;* the status, role, implication and funding of television and radio programmes of special importance should also be re-examined. Actions should also be taken to *increase radio literacy* and create a more demanding media and cultural public, to *improve the social status of self-employed and young journalists*, and to provide assistance for the creation of new forms of media organizations (social entrepreneurship).[9]

The Ministry of Culture has prepared in 2016[10] a *National Strategy for Media 2017–2024* (a part of it is a strategy for the development of national radio and TV); an extensive public discussion took place during the years 2015–2016 took place, however *it has not been enacted so far.*

44. By the number of media enrolled in the register[11] of the Ministry of Culture (hereinafter the Ministry), the Slovenian media landscape can be seen as a *cultural, ideological and substantive plural* and geographically diverse media landscape. Pluralism also depends on the media market; for this reason, the ministry *limits the concentration* of media ownership.

45. Considerable effort will be required to avoid the possibility of *political influence,* especially in the case of public media. But this influence has not been detected except for the case of the public media sector, and in the private media sector, where some owners drain once successful media companies.[12]

2. The Mission of Media in RS

46. The mission of media could be explained by definition of *public interest* in the field of media in the RS. According to the Resolution on the National Programme for Culture 2014–2017,[13] the implementation of the *Constitutional right to freedom of expression*, including the *right to public information* is in the public interest. Likewise, cultural, ideological and geographical *pluralism and diversity of media* content, the development of the Slovenian national and *cultural identity* and the Slovenian *language* and care for their visibility, the consolidation of *social values* such as basic *human rights, democracy and tolerance* (including the importance which both *social inclusion and intergenerational cooperation* for the healthy development of the company) is also in the public interest.

9. Ministry of Culture: http://www.mk.gov.si/fileadmin/mk.gov.si/pageuploads/Ministrstvo/Zakonodaja/Predpisi_v_pripravi/2013/NPK_2014-2017/Summary_NPK_2014-2017_AN.pdf.

10. http://www.mk.gov.si/fileadmin/mk.gov.si/pageuploads/Ministrstvo/Fotogalerija/2016/junij/MED-STRATStrategija_razvoja_medijev_v_Republiki_Sloveniji_do_leta_2024_-_v_1.0_junij_2016.pdf.
11. https://rmsn.ekultura.gov.si/razvid/mediji.
12. Ministry of Culture, the Resolution on the National Program for Culture 2014-2017.
13. *Ibid.*

The *Coalition Contract of the Government 2018–2022*[14] envisages the *reconstruction of media legislation* and regulation of the media space measures. *Media independence* should be strengthened by the introduction of *new forms of media organization, such as cooperatives, workers'* takeovers of media outlets or other forms of community participation in the media. One of the challenges is also to *modernize the management of RTV SLO* by strengthening the role of employees and the public and to carry out a reform of state subsidizing of media content through greater public oversight of distribution procedures and redirecting funds to direct content creators.

47. *Autonomy* of the journalistic profession, *transparency* of media ownership, *equity pluralism* and *prevention of abuse* of a dominant position in the media market is in public interest.

48. And, not least, increasing the availability of media content for *vulnerable social groups* and disabled handicapped, the existence of television and radio programmes of special interest (assuming to re- determine their importance, role, status and financing) is also public interest.[15]

49. As for media field, public interest is promotion and development of *media literacy*, the production of *high-quality media content* in the areas of arts and culture, critical reflection of society, education, science, the environment, etc., the production of high-quality media *content for children and adolescents*, the promotion of *investigative journalism*, demanding and *specific journalistic genres* and content, the existence of *high-quality general – informational newspapers*, newspapers and magazines (regardless of the media type of media content), improving the social *status of independent and young journalists* and the emergence of *new forms of media ownership* – management models.[16]

50. Ministry of Culture of the Republic of Slovenia (hereinafter RS) following the public interest in the media so far ensured *state aid* through a call for *co-financing of broadcasting media* to ensure the *diversity and pluralism* of the media landscape. But considering the situation in the media market, significant for bad business performance of the majority of media, this has not been enough so far.

3. Main Challenges in Media Policy

51. In the coming period the main challenges in the field of media policy will be *to raise the readership* of the quality general information – newspapers, journals and magazines and *to raise the quality* and increase the volume of high-quality

14. The Coalition Contract on cooperation in the LMŠ (Marjan Šarec List) Government 2018-2022: http://www.strankalms.si/wp-content/uploads/2018/08/Koalicijski-sporazum-o-sodelovanju-v-Vladi-Republike-Slovenije-za-mandatno-obdobje-2018%E2%80%932022.pdf.
15. *Ibid.*
16. *Ibid.*

media content in the areas of arts and culture, education, health, science, environment protection, etc. The challenge will also be re-examination of the *role and scope of public service* broadcasting Slovenia, enhancing *the quality of broadcasts* radio and television programmes, which are *of public interest* and to re- establish the status, role, importance and funding of radio and television programmes of special interest. One of the main challenges will also be *to raise media literacy* and the creation of complex media and culture to the public, to improve the social status of self-employed and young journalists and to aid in the creation of *new forms of media ownership* – management models (social entrepreneurship).[17]

52. In order to come up with better quality and diverse media landscape will require a *complete overhaul of media laws.* The overall objective of the media refers to the placement of Slovenia in *the Press Freedom Index* (Reporters without Borders), in which Slovenia is 2018 ranked 34th, previously 32nd.[18] The aim that by 2017 Slovenia is among the *top twenty countries has not yet realized.*

4. Media Publisher

53. A media publisher/broadcaster in Slovenia is a legal or natural person that carries out activities of disseminating programme in accordance with the Media Act (Official Gazette of the Republic of Slovenia, No. 110/06 – official consolidated text, 36/08 – ZPOmK-1, 77/10 – ZSFCJA, 90/10 – Rev. US, 87/11 – ZAvMS, 47/12, 47/15 – ZZSDT, 22/16 and 39/16, hereinafter *MMA*).[19] A publisher *independently*

---

17. *Ibid.*
18. https://rsf.org/en/slovenia.
19. The unofficial consolidated text of the Media Act includes:

   - Media Act – Zmed (Official Gazette of the Republic of Slovenia, No. 35/01 of 11 May 2001);
   - Decision to repeal Article 107 of the Media Act (Official Gazette of the Republic of Slovenia, No. 113/03 of 20 Nov. 2003);
   - Decision on the partial annulment of Article 82 of the Media Act and repealing the Rules on criteria for financing programming content of radio or television programs with status of local, regional and student significance (Official Gazette of the Republic of Slovenia, No. 16/04 of 20 Feb. 2004);
   - Decision annulling the sixth and seventh paragraphs of Article 112 of the Media Act (Official Gazette of the Republic of Slovenia, No. 123/04 of 18 Nov. 2004);
   - Radio Television Slovenia Act - ZRTVS-1 (Official Gazette of the Republic of Slovenia, No. 96/05 of 28 Oct. 2005);
   - Act Amending the Media Act - ZMed-A (Official Gazette of the Republic of Slovenia, No. 60/06 of 9 Jun. 2006);
   - Compulsory copy of publications - ZOIPub (Official Gazette of the Republic of Slovenia, No. 69/06 of 3 Jul. 2006);
   - Media Act - official consolidated text - ZMed-UPB1 (Official Gazette of the Republic of Slovenia, No. 110/06 of 26 Oct. 2006);
   - Prevention of Restriction of Competition Act - ZPOmK-1 (Official Gazette of the Republic of Slovenia, No. 36/08 of 11 Apr. 2008);
   - Act on the Slovenian Film Center, the Public Agency of the Republic of Slovenia - ZSFCJA (Official Gazette of the Republic of Slovenia, No. 77/10 of 4 Oct. 2010);

formulates the mass medium's programme concept and bears fundamental *responsibility* for the implementation thereof. The activities of a publisher may also encompass the creation or production of programme (MMA, Article 9).

The MMA (Article 9) was amended by a new third paragraph, which stipulates, that the publisher, who permits the public to comment in the media, *must formulate the rules for commenting and publish them* in a suitable place in the media. A comment that does not comply with the published rules must be withdrawn as soon as possible after the registration, or, at the latest one working day, after the registration.[20]

54. There are special conditions for founding and entering a publisher in the court register (MMA, Article 10). In order to carry out activities of disseminating programme, a legal or natural person may be founded or entered in the court register in the Republic of Slovenia if the person's head office or address of permanent residence is *located in the Republic of Slovenia,* or if the editorial board is *based in the Republic of Slovenia.*

5. Mass Media Register

55. For the purpose of entry in the mass media register, *the publisher must register the mass medium* at the ministry responsible for culture, prior to commencing the performance of activities. The following data (also any change, if/when happens) in the information needs to be filed with the application for entry in the mass media register (MMA Article 12):

- the *name* of the mass medium, the name or business name and head office address or address of permanent residence of the publisher and the *address* at which the editorial board or responsible editor is based;
- the name of the publisher's *responsible officer*, if the publisher is a legal entity and of the responsible editor;

- Decision on the finding that the second paragraph of Article 26 of the Media Act is inconsistent with the Constitution and the annulment of the judgment of the Supreme Court, the judgment of the Higher Court in Koper and the judgment of the District Court in Koper (Official Gazette of the Republic of Slovenia, No. 90/10 of 12 Nov. 2010);
- Audio-visual Media Services Act - ZAvMS (Official Gazette of the Republic of Slovenia, No. 87/11 of 2 Nov. 2011);
- Act Amending the Media Act - ZMed-B (Official Gazette of the Republic of Slovenia, No. 47/12 of 22 Jun. 2012);
- Employment, Self-Employment and Work of Aliens Act - ZZSDT (Official Gazette of the Republic of Slovenia, No. 47/15 of 30 Jun. 2015);
- Act Amending the Media Act - ZMed-C (Official Gazette of the Republic of Slovenia, No. 22/16 of 25 Mar. 2016);
- Act Amending the Media Act - ZMed-D (Official Gazette of the Republic of Slovenia, No. 39/16 of 3 June 2016).

20. The Act Amending the Media Act (ZMed-C), adopted by the National Assembly of the Republic of Slovenia at its session of 1 Mar. 2016.

- the type of mass medium and *interval of its dissemination, the method and envisaged area* of coverage for the dissemination of programme and the language of dissemination of programme;
- the sources and method of *financing and information on persons that hold ownership* or management stakes of at least 5% or stakes of at least 5% in the voting rights within the assets of a publisher of a general informative printed daily or weekly.

56. The relevant ministry *must enter a mass medium in the register if the applicant fulfils* all the conditions prescribed by the MMA, within fifteen days of receiving the application. If the applicant fails to fulfil the conditions for entry in the mass media register, the relevant ministry must, via a resolution, *deny entry* in the register. Publishers of printed mass media must send a mandatory copy of each issue to the National University Library (MMA, Article 13).

6. Ban on Performance of Activities

57. Publishers/broadcasters in Slovenia *may not disseminate programme* via a mass medium that is not entered in the mass media register at the relevant ministry (Article 16 of the MMA). The relevant inspector may in the event of an infringement of the MMA, issue a ruling on the elimination of deficiencies or irregularities determined and stipulate a deadline for the elimination thereof.

58. The relevant inspector may *prohibit a publisher/broadcaster* that is disseminating programme via a mass medium without being entered in the register from performing activities and may seize working drafts, products and materials used to perform activities.

7. Programme Concept

59. The purpose of publication and the basic substantive guidelines for the operation of a mass medium *must be set out through the programme concept* (Article 17 of the MMA).

60. The programme concept must be a *constituent part of employment contracts* between the publisher and editorial personnel and between the publisher and journalists. The special rights of editorial personnel and journalists deriving from changes or additions to the programme concept are defined by the branch collective agreement.

61. These provisions do *not apply to local, regional and student* broadcasters of television programme services if the individual programme service is intended for local inhabitants and is not included in a national network. These provisions do also not apply to television programme services specializing in telesales or self-promotion.

8. Slovenian Media Market

62. Political and economic reforms of the early 1990s following independence (including privatization) affected media market developments substantially. A number of new private radio and television broadcasters and print media appeared and made the media market more competitive and concentrated.

63. Due to a significant *decrease in advertising* for different reasons (radical political changes, economic crisis, growing competition of private media in the media market, fast development of competitive digital technology and related changes in readers' habits), Slovenian media companies in last decades, faced serious economic challenges. In addition to growing competition of private media, former socially owned media companies went through privatization processes and corporate governance restructuring, what affected their development and competitiveness significantly. Unless becoming privatized, the state (political) indirect control over former socially owned media companies remained in some of them.

64. Media analysts note that, due to the *permanent changing readership* habits caused by new online media supply, Slovenia already a decade witnesses the continuous declining circulations and readership of general informative newspapers, and magazines. The sales figures of all of the large dailies have sunk in recent years, resulting in cutbacks at the editorial offices. At the same time, the influential papers like *Delo*, *Dnevnik* and *Večer* are trying to attract more readers with the help of internet and multimedia offers. While several critical internet projects like the portal *Vest* have sprung up in recent years, serious, quality blogs are few and far between. Blogs are only rarely maintained regularly, and for the most part, do not deal with European political issues.[21]

9. Slovenian Media in Numbers

65. The number of media in the country has been rising all the time since the independence of the country in 1991. According to the Ministry of Culture, Directorate for Media (Overview of the media landscape in Slovenia, April 2014), 1,844 media types are enrolled; some media are published simultaneously in a variety of formats (print and electronic). Out of these, print media (1151) is the maximum, followed by electronic (412) Radio (116), and television (108). The *number of media outlets also grew steadily* between 2007 and 2013 (last available synthetic data), which can be seen in the following table:[22]

---

21. Milosavljević Marko, Vobič Igor, Media Landscape, Slovenia, EUROPEAN CENTER OF JOURNALISTS, ttp://ejc.net/media_landscapes/slovenia.
22. Ministry of Culture, Directorate for Media, April 2014, Overview of the media landscape in Slovenia http://www.mk.gov.si/fileadmin/mk.gov.si/pageuploads/Ministrstvo/raziskaveanalize/mediji/2014/medijska_krajina_v_sloveniji__rev_03062014.pdf.

Year	*2007*	*2008*	*2009*	*2010*	*2011*	*2012*	*2013*
Number	1,356	1,399	1,486	1,584	1,682	1,765	1,844
TV	66	69	79	86	95	102	108
Radio	105	107	110	112	113	116	116
Print	896	939	984	1036	1083	1117	1151
Electronic	163	210	236	279	324	362	412
All	*1,230*	*1,325*	*1,409*	*1,513*	*1,615*	*1,697*	*1,787*

Source: Ministry of Culture, Directorate for Media, April 2014, Overview of the media landscape in Slovenia.

66. *Media concentration in Slovenia is high.* According to Media Pluralism Monitor 2016,[23] *media ownership has been changing* at a fast pace. Majority of the print outlets have been resold to new owners due to poor financial conditions, bad management and the need for so-called restructuring. The only public broadcaster is the Radio -Television of Slovenia (RTV); the main private broadcasters are Pro Plus channels, TV3 and Planet TV.

Combined with the rise in internet usage, there have been *a lot of changes in the media landscape,* especially with daily print rapidly losing its circulation and readership. From a technical point of view, digitalization has been quite painless for Slovenia, as was the *spread of digital media.* Almost all of the population is covered by broadband, while around 70% have a cable and fixed broadband access at home.[24]

The economic crisis in 2008/2009 affected the media sector; it demonstrated the weaknesses of the existing market model of media financing.[25]

67. The Big Five among Slovenian media, according to turnover, are supposed to be three print media (Delo, Dnevnik and Večer) and two broadcast media (public service broadcaster Radiotelevizija Slovenija, 'Radio Television Slovenia' or RTV Slovenia), and a commercial broadcaster (Pro Plus), all of which have a narrow international role.[26]

B. *Television Broadcasting*

1. Public Service in Broadcasting in Slovenia

68. Public service in the field of audio-visual media services pursuant to the *Act on Radio Television Slovenia (ARTV)* (Official Gazette of the Republic of Slovenia,

23. Media Pluralism Monitor 2016, Monitoring Risks for Pluralism in the EU and Beyond, Country report: Slovenia, Milosavljević, M, Centre for Media Pluralism and Media Freedom.
24. *Ibid.*
25. *Ibid.*
26. Milosavljević Marko, Vobič Igor, Media Landscape, Slovenia, EUROPEAN CENTER OF JOURNALISTS, ttp://ejc.net/media_landscapes/slovenia.

No. 96/05, 109/05 – ZDavP-1B, 105/06 – Rev. US, 26/09 – ZIPRS0809-B and 9/14) Slov.: Zakon o Radioteleviziji Slovenija, ZRTVS-1)[27] comprises creating, producing, archiving and broadcasting informative, cultural, educational, sports, entertainment and other contents transmitted by RTV Slovenia using all available transmission technologies, either linear or non-linear.

69. RTV Slovenia's national *television networks* in accordance with the *Slovene legislation*, public service in broadcasting comprises the creation, production, archival and broadcasting of (Article 3/1 of the ARTV):

- *Two national TV* channels: TV Slovenia 1, TV Slovenia 2.
- *Three national radio* stations: Radio Slovenia 1 programme, Radio Slovenia 2 programme (Val 202), Radio Slovenia 3 programme (ARS).
- *Radio and television programmes of regional centres* in Koper and Maribor: Radio Koper, Isola Radio, TV Koper, Isola TV, Radio Maribor, Maribor, TV, Radio Budapest Hungarian minority, TV programme of the Hungarian minority in Lendava.
- *One radio and one television programme for the autochthonous Italian and Hungarian* national communities (a national program) and radio and television broadcasts for the Roma ethnic community (programmes for Roma).
- *Radio and television programmes for the Slovenian minorities* in neighbouring countries and the Slovenian emigrants and migrant workers (the contents are included in all programmes, especially in regional programmes of RTV Centre Koper).
- *Radio and television programmes for foreign audiences*: Radio Canada International (in the context of RTV Centre Maribor).
- *Teletext, web and mobile* portal: the portal MMC, MMC applications for tablets and smartphones, Mediateka for hybrid TV receivers, other applications and services.

70. Public service in addition to those programmes also includes a special national television programme called *TV Slovenia 3*. This programme is intended for

27. The unofficial consolidated text no. 4 of the Act on Radio Television Slovenia includes:

- Act on Radio Television Slovenia - ZRTVS-1 (Official Gazette of the Republic of Slovenia, No. 96/05 of 28 Oct. 2005);
- Act Amending the Tax Procedure Act - ZDavP-1B (Official Gazette RS, No. 109/05 of 6 Dec. 2005);
- Decision to annul the second paragraph of Article 15 of the Radiotelevizija Slovenija Act (Official Gazette of the Republic of Slovenia, No. 105/06 of 12 Oct. 2006);
- Act Amending the Implementation of the Budget of the Republic of Slovenia for the years 2008 and 2009 - ZIPRS0809-B (Official Gazette of the Republic of Slovenia, No. 26/09 of 6 Apr. 2009);
- Act Amending the Act on Radio Television Slovenia - ZRTVS-1A (Official Gazette of the Republic of Slovenia, No. 9/14 of 5 Feb. 2014);
- Act on Radio and Television Corporation of Slovenia (ARTV) (Off. Gazette no. 96/2005, 109/ 2005-ZDavP-1B, 105/2006 Odl.US: U-I-307/05-18, 26/2009-ZIPRS0809-B (31/2009 popr.)–consolidated text, Slov.: Zakon o Radioteleviziji Slovenija, ZRTVS-1).

live broadcasts *sessions of the National Assembly* of the Republic of Slovenia and its working bodies and playing recordings of those meetings where direct transmission is not possible. *TV Slovenia 3* offers comprehensive information to the public about all the other parliamentary developments, including meetings of the National Council of the Republic of Slovenia; it follows also the international activities of Parliament, consultations organized by the National Assembly of the Republic of Slovenia or its working bodies or the National Council of the Republic of Slovenia and other activities associated with the implementation of the Constitutional powers of the Slovenian Parliament (Article 3/2 of the ARTV).

2. General Principles of Public Broadcasting

71. When creating and preparing programmes, Radio Television Slovenia (hereinafter RTV), according to Article 3 of the ARTV:

- respect human individuality and dignity, adhere to the principles of impartiality and veracity of information as well as pluralism of opinions, world views and religion, political independence and autonomy,
- ensure the integral and impartial provision of information as well as free formation of opinions and commentaries.

3. RTV Slovenia

72. ARTV regulates the status and operation of the Radio and Television Corporation of Slovenia (hereinafter RTV Slovenia). The only founder and owner of RTV Slovenia is the *Republic of Slovenia.*

RTV Slovenia is legally bound to provide credible and impartial newscasts with which it fully informs about political developments at home and abroad, on important events in the remaining European countries, in particular EU Member States, and on important global topics, so that the provided content enables objective public information of citizens of the Republic of Slovenia, Slovenes around the world, members of Slovene national minorities in Italy, Austria and Hungary, the autochthonous Italian and Hungarian national communities in the Republic of Slovenia and the Roma community living in Slovenia (Article 4/1, 1. line of the ARTV).

73. The duty of the founder is to ensure the professional and editorial independence of RTV Slovenia, appropriate financing and suitable arrangement which serves as the basis to obtain funds for the provision of public service while respecting the financial stability of RTV Slovenia's funding sources.

74. RTV Slovenia is entered in the court register as an independent legal person of special cultural and national importance governed by public law (ARTV, Article 2).

75. The founder's rights within RTV Slovenia are exercised by the *Council of RTV* Slovenia (hereinafter: Council) unless otherwise provided for individual cases by ARTV. The Council ensures institutional autonomy and editorial independence of RTV Slovenia.

76. RTV Slovenia is the only *public, non-profit broadcasting institution* in the country (it is bound to allocate any surplus from its performance) offering public service in broadcasting media. RTV Slovenia's mission and functioning are therefore essential for satisfying the public interest in the field of radio and television in the country.

77. The legal foundation for the institution is the Law on RTV. RTV Slovenia operates both radio and television stations and programmes.

78. As it is said in the RTV Slovenia's Development Strategy 2011 – 2015, RTV Slovenia *cannot be carried out only on the basis of the market* and its mechanisms. The maximum strategic goal of RTV Slovenia is, therefore that the programme permanently ensures compliance with *public service* tasks in the field of media and that it is *financially independent.*[28]

4. RTV Slovenia's National Television Networks

79. RTV Slovenia's national *television networks* are:

- *TV Slovenia 1*: A general-interest television service with newscasts, feature films, documentaries, talk shows, series, children's programming, variety shows, and live coverage of significant national events.
- *TV Slovenia 2*: A more specialized service with programmes generally aimed at narrower audiences, sitcoms, a wide range of live sports coverage, but virtually no news.
- *TV Slovenia 3*: Specialized service dedicated to airing fully unedited proceedings of the Slovenian Parliament and Committees live, it also features documentaries, interviews and news.
- *TV Slovenia 1 HD*: TVS 1 in high-definition.
- *TV Slovenia 2 HD*: TVS 2 in high-definition.

RTV Slovenia is a full member of the European Broadcasting Union (EBU). The regional TV stations are:

- *TV Koper/Capodistria* (in Slovenian and Italian, based in Koper, received in Primorska, Istria, and parts of Friuli-Venezia Giulia via a terrestrial signal, and throughout Slovenia via cable).
- *Televizija Maribor* (in Slovenian, based in Maribor, received in northeastern Slovenia) Also has Hungarian language programming.

28. RTV Slovenia 's Development Strategy 2011–2015.

Today, television is in most cases included in bundles provided by telecommunication operators, who offer bundles with a fixed range of television stations and provide advanced features for managing TV content with digital receivers. Such user experience is based on using linear (classical), non-linear (video-on-demand), and internet services on the same platform, i.e. on the platform where until recently viewers only expected traditional TV. The following TV stations are currently broadcast via the digital terrestrial platform throughout the entire territory of the country:

- i-TV
- Kanal A
- TV Pink 3
- POP TV
- TV SLO 1
- TV SLO 2
- TV SLO 3.

In certain areas, the following programmes are also broadcast:

- RTS (east)
- Tele M (east)
- TV Koper Capodistira (west)
- TV Primorka (west)
- Vaš kanal (centre).

5. Radio and Television Programmes of Special Importance

80. In Slovenia, there are *18 radio and 11 television programmes* that have been granted the status of special importance, among them also a *student radio*, a programme with the status of a non-profit radio programme and two programmes with the status of *non-profit broadcasters*.

81. Under the mass media legislation, among them, each year, the amount of *3% of the collected contribution* to the programmes and services of RTV Slovenia should be allocated from the state budget.

82. Broadcasts produced and disseminated by radio and television programmes of special importance have been identified as the *public interest* because it significantly contributes to pluralism and diversity of media space, as well as to local population and specific target groups of listeners and viewers guarantees the exercise of the Constitutional the right to public information.

83. Broadcasts produced by the programmes of special interest also offer *complementary content of public broadcasting*, which itself through its programmes cannot even cover all the events in Slovenia, and thus fill the information gap on the axis of the local – national.

84. As the Ministry of Culture of the Republic of Slovenia (Ministry) notes in the Resolution on the National Programme for Culture 2014–2017, most of the programmes of particular interest find themselves in difficult financial straits because of highly *market-oriented competition and decline in advertising* revenue.

85. Ministry further notes that it is obvious that the current system of granting the status of programmes of special interest and financing of limited budgetary resources through annual calls does *not provide optimal solutions* for sustainable existence of radio and television broadcasts, which are of the public interest.[29]

86. It is further said in the strategy, that due to negative effects of the economic crisis, the programmes are only *fighting for their survival* and consequently extremely difficult meet the imposed legal obligations or carry out its mission in the public interest; this situation calls for serious reflection on the role and status of programmes of special importance to preserve of Slovenian national and cultural identity, achieve the highest ethical and professional standards, in particular in the field of journalism and more even territorial distribution of radio and television programmes, which are in the public interest. The first step to a more permanent solution that will provide a *stable source of funding* and long-term way of radio and television broadcasts that are in the public interest, the definition of programmes of particular interest as an extension of the public service of RTV Slovenia.[30]

6. Private Television

87. According to the *register led by the Agency for communication network and services* of the Republic of Slovenia (hereinafter: the Agency),[31] 86 television programmes (public and private) are registered in Slovenia.[32]

88. The Republic of Slovenia has no ownership share in any of the private digital media. The Republic of Slovenia is the owner of the Triglav Insurance Company, which is the majority owner of Triglav naložbe, finančna družba d.d., which, in turn, owns a minority share in the Info TV television company.

89. *Pro Plus* is the leading private Television broadcasting company in Slovenia. The company runs 2 channels, Pop TV and Kanal A. Pop TV has long been

29. Ministry of Culture of the Republic of Slovenia, the Resolution on the National Program for Culture 2014–2017.
30. *Ibid.*
31. http://www.akos-rs.si/radio-and-television channels?search=search&page=1&vrsta_postaje=tv&imetnik=-1&program_ra=-1&stDovoljenje_ra=-1&status_ra=-1&program_tv=-1&stDovoljenje_tv=-1&status_tv=-1.
32. Data referring to ownership structure are of course changeable during the time and could at a later stage be different.

the market leader in the country but has begun to be challenged by the arrival of other competitors. The pop TV broadcasts also a lot of local productions.[33]

90. Television stations *POP TV* (highest ratings in Slovenia) and *KANAL A* are owned by the companies POP TV d.o.o. and KANAL A d.o.o. The companies have a common owner, the PRODUKCIJA PLUS d.o.o. Production Company, which is wholly owned by Central European Media Enterprises LTD registered in the Bermuda Islands.[34]

7. Shares of Slovenian and European Audio-Visual Works

91. Broadcasters report to the Agency for communication network and services of the Republic of Slovenia each year until the end of February to provide disaggregated data on the proportion of European audio-visual works in the annual transmission time for the previous year.

92. Within this proportion separately must be shown data on the extent of the annual transmission time, data on the share of own production, Slovenian audio-visual works and audio-visual works of independent producers and data on the proportion of new audio-visual works.

93. According to the AKOS[35] 2017 Annual Report, the register of television broadcasting holders reveals that seventy legal and natural persons held eighty-nine valid television broadcasting licenses at the end of 2017. Nine of those hold more than one license, and these nine together hold a total of twenty-eight licenses, which comprises one-third of valid licenses. Furthermore, thirty-one have active rights to disseminate television programming in digital broadcasting technology.[36]

Five new licenses for television activities were issued for the following TV channels: PLANET TV 2 and PLANET PLUS, published by Antena TV SL d.o.o., Ljubljana TV, published by TV LJUBLJANA d.o.o., TRŽIČ TV, published by Vprašaj d.o.o., and MOJKANAL, published by Mojkanal institute. Of the new licenses for television activities, one was issued for themed television programming, namely Planet Plus.[37]

At the request of license holders, four licenses for conducting television activities were altered. Three of them were changed into licenses for themed television programming, namely POP OTO, POP KINO and POP BRIO, all published by POP TV d.o.o. At the end of 2017, there were a total of four licenses for the med television programming. In 2017, eight declaratory decisions on the expiration of the

33. C21 Media, 2008. CME - Broadcaster Profile – Pro Plus – Slovenia: http://www.cetv-net.com/en/press-center/media/49.shtml; http://arts1091.unsw.wikispaces.net/Slovenia%202012.
34. The data on ownership could change during the time and therefore are not necessary accurate.
35. AKOS – Agency for communication networks of Slovenia.
36. AKOS Annual Report 2017: https://www.akos-rs.si/files/APEK_eng/About_APEK/Annual_reports/AKOS-annual-report-2017.pdf.
37. *Ibid.*

validity of a license for conducting television activities were issued. Throughout the year, seven licenses were transferred to new publishers.[38]

In Slovenia, smart TVs in households are still a low percentage, compared to the EU average (49.7 %), as it stands at 36.1 %, of the existing smart TVs not connected to the internet. Slovenian viewers watch television on a TV set, with only 8% using mobile TV services, while 7.8 % watch television programming over the internet on devices such as tablets, smartphones, and computers.[39]

C. Radio

1. Public Radio Broadcasting

94. The Radio and Television Slovenia (RTV Slovenia), the public broadcasting organization, broadcasts the following public radio programmes: Val 202, Radio Slovenija, Radio Koper, Radio Maribor, Pomurski madžarski radio, Radio ARS and Radio Slovenia International.

95. RTV Slovenia's *national radio networks* are based in Ljubljana and broadcast in Slovene. The radio programmes are the following:

- *Prvi programme* (first programme): A general radio broadcasting service carrying news and news reports, a variety of specialized broadcasts, and a wide range of music.
- *Val 202*: A popular music-oriented service with the emphasis on pop and rock music, news bulletins and updates, talk segments, lifestyle reports, and live sports coverage.
- *ARS*: A cultural service concentrating on classical music, radio drama, and other cultural programming.

96. RTV Slovenia's *regional* radio stations are based in regional RTV centres, and broadcast in Slovenian and/or the languages of the indigenous minorities in the area. They can be heard only in their own regions. The regional radio stations that belong to RTV Slovenia are:

- *Radio Koper* (in Slovenian, based in Koper, received in the Slovenian Littoral);
- *Radio Capodistria* (in Italian, based in Koper, received in Friuli-Venezia Giulia, Slovenian Littoral, and Istria);
- *Radio Maribor* (in Slovenian, based in Maribor, received in northeastern Slovenia);
- *MMR – Pomurski madžarski radio* (Hungarian: *Muravidéki Magyar Rádió*) (broadcasting in Hungarian with Hungarian folk and mostly pop music, based in RTV Maribor's Lendava studio, received in Prekmurje).

---

38. *Ibid.*
39. *Ibid.*

97. Radio Slovenia International (RSI; in English and German) IS based in Maribor, heard in various places around Slovenia and southeastern Austria; for expatriates, tourists, English-speaking Slovenians, and foreigners.

2. Private Radio Broadcasting

98. According to the registrar at the Agency *116 radio programmes* (public and private) are registered in Slovenia.[40]

Analogue FM radio is still a very popular way of broadcasting. Cheap transmission equipment, simple computerized production and broadcasting, and simple and cheap radios have contributed to the wide use of this technology. However, it takes more than just technical equipment to set up a radio station.[41]

Even though analogue FM radio is still the prevailing radio broadcasting technology, the possibility of digital radio networks already exists. The VHF (band III, 174–230 MHz) and L bands (1452–1490 MHz) of the radio spectrum have been allocated for this purpose. The prevailing technology for digital radio networks is T-DAB; however, other systems are also being examined. The possibilities and technologies for digitalizing the radio spectrum band currently used for FM radio (87.5–108 MHz) are also being examined.[42]

99. The Republic of Slovenia has no ownership share in any private radio station in Slovenia. A substantial difference between the private and public media is in the superiority of profit as a goal over the public service in the case of private media. Apart from Radio Slovenia and three regional public radio stations, as a part of RTV Slovenia, as the national radio broadcaster, all other are private, commercial radio stations.

100. Slovenia's largest private (commercial) radio station is Radio City, owned by Radio City d.o.o., owned wholly by Mišo Hoelbl. The second is Radio Hit, owned by R Domžale d.o.o., owned by Stane and Vanda Cencelj. The third is Radio 1, owned by Radio 1 d.o.o., owned by the Infonet media company, Boštjan Protner, Leopold Oblak and other small shareholders.[43]

---

40. *See*: http://www.akos-rs.si/radio-and-television channels?search=search&page=2&vrsta_postaje=ra&imetnik=-1&program_ra=-1&stDovoljenje_ra=-1&status_ra=-1&program_tv=-1&stDovoljenje_tv=-1&status_tv=-1#obroba.
41. https://www.akos-rs.si/analog-radio.
42. https://www.akos-rs.si/digital-radio-networks.
43. Data referring to ownership structure are changeable and could be different during the time.

D. *Print Media*

1. General on Print Media in Slovenia

101. Slovenian print media market is *linguistically and geographically relatively small.* The most of print media are those that appear less than four times a year (655), followed by sleepwalkers (264), quarterly (105), bimonthly (48), weekly (45) blogs (8), at least we biweeklies (3). But these numbers say nothing about the development, pluralism, diversity, equity transparency and professionalism of the media space. Apparently the Slovenian media market is active and numerically abundant, but most of the media are at the edge of survival.[44]

102. The Republic of Slovenia has *no direct ownership shares* in the printed media. Indirectly, it owns smaller shares in *Večer* (10%) through the Slovenska odškodninska družba (SOD – Slovenian Compensation Company), in Dnevnik (2.67%) through Mobitel, and in Primorske novice (30.77%) through Luka Koper, Hit and Intereuropa.[45]

103. According to the Ministry of Culture, in Slovenia, there are currently *915 printed media,* of which 7 are dailies, 43 weeklies and 57 biweeklies. Printed media can be classified according to several categories (*daily newspapers, periodical press, weeklies and mass circulation* free press).

2. Daily Newspapers

DELO[46]

104. Delo d.d. publishing house is said to be the most important media company in Slovenia. *Delo* is the largest and one of the oldest national daily newspaper in Slovenia, with its average daily print run being around 61,000 issues (which claims almost half of all newspapers being distributed (Culture Si 2012) (Press Reference 2012).[47] The data on printing, however, changes constantly.

105. Delo Publishing House (in English, delo means 'labour') is a public limited liability company that employs around 450 people, 200 in the journalist section (170 journalists, 9 in the cultural section) and others in the service sector (distribution, marketing and printing). Delo publishes the daily newspaper Delo, with 4 magazine supplements (Deloindom, Ona, Polet, Vikend). Other publications are the daily tabloid Slovenske novice; the Sunday newspaper Nedelo, the Pogledi Newspaper on art, culture and society, and the specialized magazine Grafičar (graphic

44. Milosavljević Marko, Vobič Igor, Media Landscape, Slovenia, European Center of Journalists, ttp://ejc.net/media_landscapes/slovenia.
45. Data referring to ownership structure are changeable and could vary greatly overtime.
46. *See*: http://dd.delo.si/kdosmo.
47. http://arts1091.unsw.wikispaces.net/Slovenia%202012.

industry). Delo Publishing House is also running three internet portals Delo.si, Slovenskenovice.si and Pogledi.si as well as recognized annual events. Additionally, Delo's content is now available on mobile and tablet platforms.[48] The data on programmes and publications, however, change constantly.

106. Media company Delo d.o.o. has been, since 2015, 100% owned by FMR.[49]

107. Delo d.d. publishes two leading dailies: Slovenske novice, (circulation of 100,624 copies) and Delo (76,341 copies). Delo d.d. also publishes Nedelo weekly (circulation 57,339) and supplements Ona (170,250 copies), Vikend (212,371), Delo in dom (165,129), Polet (163,058) and Delo FT (74.550), Mag weekly (15,227) and free Total Tedna (375,000).[50]

108. Delo d.d. company also has significant shares in the following media:[51]

1	RADIO PTUJ (radio station)	10%
2	ŠTAJERSKI TEDNIK (printed media – weekly)	10%
3	MARIBORSKE NOVICE (printed media – weekly)	10%
4	VEČER (printed media – daily)	20%
5	7DNI (printed media – weekly)	20%
6	GORENJSKI GLAS (printed media – weekly)	10%
7	RADIO IN (radio station)	10%

DNEVNIK

109. Dnevnik d.d. newspaper company is considered the second biggest media company in the country.

110. Dnevnik is one of the three biggest Slovenian print media companies, founded originally as the *Ljubljanski Dnevnik* by Liberation Front of the Slovene People, and then later, being renamed in 1968. The daily *Dnevnik* is a newspaper that focuses on national general interest, informing its audience 'every day in a concise, ordered and authentic way about what is happening in all fields of life' (Publicitas 2012). In 2006, *Dnevnik*'s circulation ran between 50,000 and 70,000 copies per day; however, in 2011, the daily print run was approximately 52,000. In 2009, the National Research on Readership found that the *Dnevnik* was read by 111,000

48. http://www.culture.si/en/Delo_Publishing_House.
49. The ownership structure of companies can change during the time and it is not necessarily accurate at the time being.
50. Data from 2014.
51. The ownership structure of companies changes relatively fast over time, so that these numbers do not necessarily reflect their shares in the near future.

people giving the newspaper a reach of 6.5% (Culture Si 2012).[52] The data on circulation, however, change constantly; some of the current data are available at the end of this chapter.

Its ownership structure in 2014 was as follows:[53]

1	DZS, D.D.	35.11%
2	DZS Investicije d.o.o.	15.94%
2	STYRIA MEDIA INTERNATIONAL AG	25.74%
3	DELO PRODAJA, D.D.	10.35%
4	ČZP VEČER D.D.	6.52%
5.	The rest	6.34%

(Delo prodaja d.d. is indirectly controlled by DZS, and so are numerous small shareholders – employees of Dnevnik and DZS)

111. Dnevnik d.d. newspaper company publishes daily newspaper Dnevnik, (circulation of 58.391 copies), daily Direkt (circulation 18.000), weeklies Nedeljski Dnevnik (137.850), Hopla (26,510) and Dnevnikov objektiv (58,391), and supplements Pilot (186,585), Nika (200,000), Moj dom (200,000) Antena (68,000), Moje zdravje (80,000) and Denar&Svet nepremičnin (80,000).[54]

112. Dnevnik d.d. had in 2014 the following ownership shares in other Slovenian media:[55]

1	VESTNIK (printed media – weekly)	18.25%
2	RADIO MURSKI VAL (radio station)	18.25%
3	PRIMORSKE NOVICE (printed media – daily)	12.10%
4	GORIŠKA (printed media – monthly)	12.10%
5	DIREKT (printed media – daily)	100%
7	ARSVITA D.O.O. (owner of Delo–revije)	Not known

113. The owner of Dnevnik d.d., DZS d.d., had in 2014 the following ownership shares in other media:[56]

52. Publicitas, 2012. – Dnevnik (Slovenia): http://www.publicitas.com/belgium/represented-media/fact sheet/?PARAM1=DMEDL1&title=DNEVNIK%2B(SLOVENIA; http://arts1091.unsw.wikispaces.n et/Slovenia%202012.
53. The ownership structure of companies can change during the time and it is not necessarily accurate at the time being.
54. Data are from 2014.
55. The ownership structure of companies can change during the time and it is not necessarily accurate at the time being.
56. The ownership structure of companies can change during the time and it is not necessarily accurate at the time being.

1	RADIO BREŽICE (radio station)	10%

114. Through a network of companies and individuals DZS d.d. also controls Delo prodaja d.d. company, by far the largest distributor of printed press in Slovenia, distributing over 10 million of newspapers and magazines every month through its over 140 newsagents.

VEČER

115. Večer d.d. newspaper and publishing company is considered the third biggest in the country. Večer, the third largest of the three major media publications in Slovenia, was established in 1945 and is published in Maribor, Slovenia. It wasn't until 1949 that the newspaper was published daily and in 1952, underwent a name change from *Vestnik* to its current title. It is the most important newspaper in the central and northeast region of Slovenia because of the priority it gives to local events in that region. It is a regional, general-interest newspaper and covers national and international current affairs, including opinions, news, politics, sports, culture, business, economy, labour and employment. In 2011, Večer's print run was 45,000 daily. In 2009, it was read by 123,000 people giving Večer a reach of 7.2%. Delo currently holds 80% of shares of Večer.[57] Current numbers are obviously different (please see some of them at the end of this chapter).

116. Its ownership structure in 2014 was as follows:[58]

Delo d.d.	Dunajska cesta 5	1000 Ljubljana	79,2376 %
Delo Prodaja, d.d.	Dunajska cesta 5	1000 Ljubljana	6,9392 %
Slovenska odškodninska družba, d.d.	Mala ulica 5	1000 Ljubljana	9,9998 %
Info Holding, d.d.- v stečaju	Titiova cesta 2/A	2000 Maribor	0,0070 %
Small shareholders			3,8164 %

117. Večer d.d.publishes Večer daily newspaper (circulation of 53,000 copies), weekly supplement Kvadrati (53,000), Bombon weekly (72,000), TV Večer (68,700), 7DNI weekly (9,500 copies), Naš dom weekly (10,000), Vroči kaj monthly (5,000 copies).[59]

57. Ad native, 2012, Media Represented Vecer Slovenia: http://www.adnative.net/germany/represented media/factsheet/?PARAM1=VM6VM1; http://arts1091.unsw.wikispaces.net/Slovenia%202012.
58. The ownership structure of companies can change during the time and it is not necessarily accurate at the time being.
59. Data from 2014.

PRIMORSKE NOVICE

118. Primorske Novice d.o.o. publishes Primorske novice daily newspaper (25,000) and Goriška monthly (25,000).

The ownership structure of Primorske novice d.o.o. in 2014 was as follows:[60]

1	BANKA KOPER D.D.	17.12%
2	PRIMORJE D.D.	16.92%
3	DNEVNIK D.D.	12.10%
4	LUKA KOPER D.D.	10.83%
5	KB 1909	10.81%
6	INTEREUROPA D.D.	10%
7	HIT D.D.	9.94%
8	FORMA INN KOPER	7.09%

The Republic of Slovenia does not own shares. However, companies in the majority ownership of the state (Luka Koper, Intereuropa, Hit) do own them, but they do not have a controlling stake.

FINANCE

119. Finance d.o.o. publishes the daily newspaper Finance, monthly Manager and Moje finance.

The ownership structure of Časnik Finance d.o.o. in 2014 was as follows:[61]

1	BONNIER BUSINESS PRESS, ŠVEDSKA	100%

3. Periodical Press

Delo-revije d.d.

120. Slovenia's leading publisher of magazines and leisure publications with an annual output of 12,000,000 copies of 19 magazines, 7 special issues, 7 regular supplements, books and booklets (data 2014).

60. The ownership structure of companies can change during the time, and it is not necessarily accurate at the time being.
61. The ownership structure of companies can change during the time, and it is not necessarily accurate at the time being.

121. The company's ownership structure in 2014 was as follows:[62]

1	ARSVITA D.O.O.	50.72%
2	ALPRESS D.O.O. LJUBLJANA	28.14%
3	RA – FI INŽENIRING, D.O.O., LJUBLJANA	3.54%
4	KLADARIN LENČA	2.57%
5	GUZEJ TINE	2.57%

122. Delo-revije d.d. publishes Slovenia's leading magazines, including Jana, Lady, Obrazi, Stop, Anja, Eva, Kih, Smrklja, Modna Jana, Ambient, Lepa in zdrava, Naša žena, Zdravje, Pri nas doma, Rože & Vrt, Moj mikro, Lady Križanke, Joker, Dobra kuhinja, Non-stop, Telekomunikacije, Ljubezenske zgodbe Lady and Naravna zdravila.

ADRIA MEDIA LJUBLJANA D.O.O.

123. Adria Media Ljubljana d.o.o. is Slovenia's second largest magazine publisher. Adria Media Ljubljana is a subsidiary of Adria Media Holding and Styria Medien International, which are also present in Croatia and Serbia.

The company's ownership structure in 2013 was as follows:

1	ADRIA MEDIA HOLDING GMBH, GERMANY (GRUNER + JAHR GMBH) (SANOMA MAGAZINES)	75%
2	STYRIA MEDIA INTERNATIONAL AG	25%

124. The company published thirteen magazines: Avto magazin, Connect, Cosmopolitan, Elle, Geo, Lea, Lisa, Lisa – Čarovnija okusa, Lisa – Moje stanovanje, Men's Health, Moj lepi vrt, Nova and Playboy. Annually, Adria Media Ljubljana d.o.o. issues over 6,000,000 copies of magazines and prints over 25,000,000 preview pages.[63] This data are constantly changeable.

4. Weeklies

125. Mladina is one of the most important political weeklies, with a circulation of 19,000. It is published by Mladina d.d. in which the largest individual owner is the Italian financial company KB1909.

62. The ownership structure of companies can change during the time, and it is not necessarily accurate at the time being.
63. Data are from 2014.

126. *Mag* is Slovenia's second most important political weekly, with a circulation of 16,000 copies. Mag is published by Delo d.d.

5. Mass Circulation Free Dailies and Weeklies

127. The data on weeklies' circulation (as of any other media) are interesting just as an orientation; however, the data change constantly and are therefore not accurate at the time. The largest among them is *Total tedna* published by Delo d.d., in which Pivovarna Laško d.d. has the majority share. Total tedna has a circulation of 375,000 copies.

128. Slovenia's second largest free weekly is *Dobro jutro*, with a circulation of 350,000 copies. It is published by Regionalni mediji d.o.o., a company owned by Dija mediji d.o.o. and Austrian Media Sud-Ost Beratungs.

129. The third in line is *Žurnal*, with a circulation of 250,000 copies, published by Žurnal media d.o.o., a company owned by Austria's Styria Medien International AG.

6. Average Number of Readers

130. Data on the readership of Slovene printed media *differ a lot depending on the issuer* of the publication of data. For example *New research of readership, Večer, 2018,* shows that readership of the five biggest printed media in Slovenia of 2018,[64] the printed editions of all diaries – Večer, Dnevnik, Delo, Finance and Slovenske novice – *reach 475,000 readers* who read at least one newspaper. *Readability data for 2018*, according to this source, shows the following picture:

- Slovenske novice 306,300
- Delo 153,900
- Dnevnik 107,900
- Večer 107,900
- Finance 80,300.

However, Slovenian Advertising Association's Table shows the following picture for the number of *printed copies for 2017:*

- Slovenske novice 65.980
- Delo 34.696
- Dnevnik 26.166
- Večer 22.933
- Finance 7.829.

64. New research of readership (Valicon), Večer, 2018: https://www.vecer.com/tiskani-mediji-imajo-doseg-in-tezo-6609405.

E. Concluding Remarks

131. As it is foreseen in the National Programme for Culture 2014–2017, adopted in 2013, Slovenia envisages adopting a separate *media strategy for 2015–2020*; measures and actions will be proposed to *increase the readership* of general–interest newspapers and magazines providing information, and to boost the *quality and volume of media content* in areas such as culture and arts, education and training, health, science, protection of the environment, etc.[65]

132. In the field of broadcasting media, it is foreseen that the *role and scope of the public radio and television* network will be examined; radio and television programmes that are in the public interest will be given additional support; the status, role, implication and funding of television and radio programmes of special importance will also be re-examined; actions will be taken to increase *radio literacy* and create a more *demanding media and cultural public*; to improve the social status of self-employed and young *journalists,* and to provide assistance for the creation of new forms of media organizations (social entrepreneurship).[66]

133. The National Programme for Culture 2014–2017 provides for a key general goal in this field to see Slovenia among the first twenty countries on the Press Freedom Index by 2017; however, this goal has not been yet achieved.

II. Technical Infrastructure

A. The Meaning of Infrastructure

134. Components of broadcasting infrastructure that exist in public and private broadcasting system of Slovenia are legally defined and regulated by several pieces of legislation in Slovenia, mostly in the Electronic Communications Act (Official Gazette of the Republic of Slovenia, Nos 109/12, 110/13, 40/14 – ZIN-B, 54/14 – Rev. US, 81/15 and 40/17) (hereinafter *ECA)*[67] and the Act on Digital Broadcasting (Official Gazette of the Republic of Slovenia, Nos 102/07, 85/10, 47/12 and 109/12 – ZEKom-1) (hereinafter *DBA*).[68]

---

65. The National Program for Culture 2014–2017, adopted in 2013 by the National Assembly at the proposal of the government, contains development goals and measures to unlock development potential in different areas, and establish culture as an essential factor of development of both the individual and society.
66. *Ibid.*
67. The unofficial consolidated text of the Electronic Communications Act comprises:

   - Electronic Communications Act - ZEKom-1 (Official Gazette of the Republic of Slovenia, No. 109/12 of 31 Dec. 2012);
   - Act Amending and Supplementing the Electronic Communications Act - ZEKom-1A (Official Gazette of the Republic of Slovenia, No. 110/13 of 27 Dec. 2013);
   - Act Amending the Inspection Supervision Act - ZIN-B (Official Gazette of the Republic of Slovenia, No. 40/14 of 3 Jun. 2014);

ECA regulates the *conditions for the provision of electronic communications* networks and the provision of electronic communications services (Article 1 of the ECA).

DBA regulates digital broadcasting, *conditions for the implementation of digital broadcasting, rights and obligations* of performers, changes in the management of the radio frequency spectrum, gradual transition from analogue to digital broadcasting, integration and introduction of complementary and innovative services and gradual shutdown of analogue broadcasting and incentive measures, intended to speed up the transition to digital broadcasting (Article 1 of the DBA).

135. ECA and DBA define several terms that could be understood as the infrastructure necessary *for radio and television broadcasting* and explain the expression *broadcasting* itself. Following, we present some (far from comprehensive) definitions of basic terms of the broadcasting infrastructure (most of them in Article 3 of the ECA).

136. In addition, in this chapter, we describe the basic *institutions* in the field of broadcasting infrastructure, which are according to the legislation authorized to regulate, concern about and supervise the field.

B. The Term 'Broadcasting'

137. According to ECA, *broadcasting* means a radio communications service in which the transmission and distribution of radio or television programmes are

---

- Decision to repeal Articles 162, 163, 164, 165, 166, 167, 168 and 169 of the Electronic Communications Act (Official Gazette of the Republic of Slovenia, No. 54/14 of 18 Jul. 2014);
- Act Amending the Electronic Communications Act - ZEKom-1B (Official Gazette of the Republic of Slovenia, No. 81/15 of 30 Oct. 2015);
- Act Amending the Electronic Communications Act - ZEKom-1C (Official Gazette of the Republic of Slovenia, No. 40/17 of 21 Jul. 2017);
- Electronic Communications Act (Official Gazette No. 43/2004, 86/2004-ZVOP-1, 129/2006, 13/2007-UPB1, 102/2007-ZDRad, 110/2009, 33/2011, 109/2012-ZEKom-1, ECA, Slov.: Zakon o elektronskih komunikacijah, ZEKom UPB1 (Official Gazette of RS, no. 13/07 dated 15 Feb. 2007).

68. The unofficial consolidated text of the Digital Broadcasting Act encompasses:

- Digital Broadcasting Act - ZDRad (Official Gazette of the Republic of Slovenia, No. 102/07 of 9.11.2007) and
- Act Amending the Digital Broadcasting Act - ZDRad-A (Official Gazette of the Republic of Slovenia, No. 85/10 of 29 Oct. 2010);
- Act Amending the Digital Broadcasting Act - ZDRad-B (Official Gazette of the Republic of Slovenia, No. 47/12 of 22 Jun. 2012);
- Electronic Communications Act - ZEKom-1 (Official Gazette of the Republic of Slovenia, No. 109/12 of 31 Dec. 2012);
- Digital Broadcasting Act (Official Gazette of RS, no. 102/07 dated 9 Nov. 2007, DBA, Slov.: Zakon o digitalni radiodifuziji.

intended for direct public reception in open space without the choice of selection. The term 'programme' has the same meaning as ascribed to it in the MMA.

138. Under DBA (Article 3, p. 1), digital broadcasting is a radio communication service intended for terrestrial digital broadcasting and broadcasting of radio or television programmes with direct public reception in an open space.

139. DBA (Article 3, p. 1) defines *digital broadcasting* as radio communications service in which the digital terrestrial transmission and dissemination of radio or television programming are intended for direct, open-space reception by the general public. The design of the digital broadcasting networks must be *frequency-based* in such a way as to enable the most efficient use of the radio frequency spectrum in accordance with known technological options. In particular, the frequency planning of networks should be based on the use of *radio frequency spectrum* by single-frequency networks, if possible (DBA, Article 4).

140. *Innovative services,* according to DBA, are services offered in a multiplex system which are not intended for digital transmission and dissemination of television or radio programming. *Complementary services* are services linked to television or radio programmes transmitted digitally and disseminated in a multiplex system that can be technologically and reasonably provided along with television or radio programming (DBA Article 3, §§2 and 3).

C. Electronic Communications

141. In addition to governing the conditions for ensuring an electronic communications *network* and for the provision of electronic communications *services,* the ECA ensures *universal service,* management of the *radio frequency spectrum* and the use of number space *(numbering).*

142. In addition, the ECA lays down the conditions for *restrictions on ownership rights*, defines the *rights of users, governs* the operation of networks and services in emergency situations, governs the *protection of secrecy and confidentiality* of electronic communications, governs the *resolution of disputes* among subjects in the electronic communications markets, governs the responsibilities and tasks of the relevant Agency of the RS as an independent regulative body as well as the powers of other bodies operating under ECA (ECA Article 3).

D. Electronic Communication Network

143. Electronic communications network, according to ECA (Article 3), means transmission systems and, where applicable, switching or routing equipment. The network includes other resources like:

- *inactive network elements*, which permit the conveyance of signals by *wire, radio, optical* or other electromagnetic means;
- *satellite networks*, fixed (circuit- and packet-switched, including internet) and mobile terrestrial networks, electricity cable systems (to the extent that they are used for the purpose of transmitting signals);
- *networks used for radio and television broadcasting, and cable television* (CATV) networks, irrespective of the type of information conveyed.

144. *'Broadband network'* is a public communications network that enables the transmission of data at high speed.

E. Electronic Communications Equipment

145. *Electronic communications equipment* is under ECA (Article 3) all the associated facilities of electronic communications networks that enable electronic communications services. They include, inter alia, the switching and routing equipment or all types of base stations or electrical cable systems, when they are used for the purpose of:

- *transmitting signals in the provision of electronic communications services*;
- *radio and television broadcasting and CATV* and cable communications, irrespective of the type of information conveyed.

F. Electronic Communications Service

146. An electronic communications service comprises wholly or mainly the transmission of signals by electronic communications networks, including telecommunications services and transmission services on networks used for broadcasting. An electronic communications service does *not include:*

- services that provide or carry out *editorial control* of content transmitted via electronic communications networks or electronic communications services;
- *information society services* that do not include wholly or mainly transmission of signals by electronic communications networks (ECA Article 3);
- any service that is not normally implemented *against payment.*

G. The Prescribed Minimum Set of Services

147. The prescribed *minimum set of services* of a certain quality is available to all end-users in the Republic of Slovenia under affordable prices irrespective of their geographical location. The minimum set of services, falling within the thus designated universal service, includes:

- a connection to the *public telephone network* and provision of access to publicly available telephone services at a fixed location in response to reasonable requests by the users, capable of allowing end-users to make and receive local, national and international telephone calls, transmission of facsimile communications and data communications, at data rates that are sufficient to *permit functional internet access*;
- ensuring and providing access to *universal service* for the provision of information on subscribers ('universal directory service') in accordance with Article 12 of ECA (relocation or modification of other installations and the subsequent construction of other installations);
- ensuring *public telephone boxes* where users can dial, free of charge and without the use of any means of payment, *the numbers for emergency calls* with a view to meet the reasonable needs of end-users in terms of the geographical coverage, the number of public telephone boxes, the accessibility of such telephones to disabled users and the quality of services;
- ensuring *measures for the disabled end-users* that will enable the disabled end-users appropriate access to and use of publicly available telephone services, including the same access to emergency services, directories and directory services from which benefit other end-users.

148. ECA defines the term 'by electronic means'; it means that the service is sent initially and received at its destination by means of electronic equipment for the processing (including digital compression) and storage of data, and is entirely transmitted, conveyed and received by wire, radio, optical means or other electromagnetic means

H. Electronic Signature

149. Electronic Commerce and Electronic Signature Act (Official Gazette of the Republic of Slovenia, No. 98/04 – official consolidated text, 61/06 – ZEPT and 46/14) (hereinafter *ECESA*)[69] regulates *electronic business*, which covers business

69. The unofficial consolidated text of the Electronic Commerce and Electronic Signature Act comprises:

- Electronic Commerce and Electronic Signature Act - ZEPEP (Official Gazette of the Republic of Slovenia, No. 57/00 of 23 Jun. 2000);
- Act Amending the Act on the Organization and Work of the Ministries - ZODPM-C (Official Gazette of the Republic of Slovenia, No. 30/01 of 26.04.2001)l
- Act Amending the Electronic Commerce and Electronic Signature Act - ZEPEP-A (Official Gazette of the Republic of Slovenia, No. 25/04 of 19 Mar. 2004);
- Act Amending the Law on Notaries - ZN-C (Official Gazette of the Republic of Slovenia, No. 73/04 of 5 Jul. 2004);
- Electronic Commerce and Electronic Signature Act - official consolidated text - ZEPEP-UPB1 (Official Gazette of the Republic of Slovenia, No. 98/04 of 9 Sep. 2004);
- Electronic Commerce Act on the Market - ZEPT (Official Gazette of the Republic of Slovenia, No. 61/06 of 13.06.2006);

in electronic form through the application of information and communication technologies and the use of electronic signatures in legal transactions.

150. This also includes the electronic operation of *judicial, administrative* and other procedures, unless provided otherwise by law.

I. Cable Penetration and Audio-Visual Market

151. Cable ducts, according to ECA, means a horizontal civil engineering structure consisting of ducts, pipes and the like that facilitate the setting-up and maintenance of telecommunications conduits. Cable is the most important distribution platform serving more than 30% of homes at the end of 2012. The main operator is Telemach (Mid Europa Partners), which had almost 200,000 subscribers in 2012. *Telemach* is the leading Slovenian provider of CATV, telephony and broadband internet services. The company is providing an extensive network based on a combination of optical and coaxial components.

152. According to MAVISE database for Slovenia, *updated in July 2017,*[70] there are 74 TV channels established in the country, 78 foreign TV channels targeting the country, 226 other TV channels available in the country, 21 local TV channels established in the country, 10 on-demand audio-visual services established in the country, 66 foreign on-demand audio-visual services targeting the country. Among operators (all types of companies), there are 77 broadcasters, 8 providers of on-demand audio-visual services, 3 distributors, transmitters and/or packagers and no internet/mobile packager in Slovenia.

§3. Service Provider Media Group

I. Institutional Infrastructure

A. Electronic Communications Council of the RS

153. Article 229 of the ECA sets out the *Electronic Communications Council (ECC)* of the RS (hereinafter: the Council); it is a body charged with *providing advice for directing the development* of electronic communications and protecting the interests of consumers in the area of electronic communications in the RS.

– Act Amending and Supplementing the Electronic Commerce and Electronic Signature Act - ZEPEP-B (Official Gazette of the Republic of Slovenia, No. 46/14 of 23 Jun. 2014.

The Electronic Commerce and Electronic Signature Act (ECESA), Slovene: Zakon o elektronskem poslovanju in elektronskem podpisu – ZEPEP (Official Gazette No. 57/2000 of 23. 6. 2000, as amended by ZODPM-C (Official Gazette No. 30/01 of 26. 4. 2001and ZEPEP-A, Official Gazette No. 25/04 of 19. 3. 2004) ZODPM-C (Uradni list RS, št. 30/01 of26. 4 . 2001) in

70. http://mavise.obs.coe.int/country?id=27.

154. It has 11 members, who are *appointed by the National Assembly* for a period of five years. Four members are appointed from among the representatives of consumer organizations, representative disabled organizations (at the proposal of the National Council for Disabled Organizations) and educational institutions, with at least one member being appointed from each of these organizations. The remaining seven members are various experts in the area of electronic communications.

155. Tasks of the Council are regulated by Article 231 of the ECA. According to ECA *the Council produces opinions, recommendations and proposals* regarding matters in the area of electronic communications, including the protection of consumers, the disabled and users with special social needs in this area. The *Agency may request the opinion of the Council* regarding matters relating to electronic communications. The Agency publishes the opinions, recommendations and proposals on its website.

B. Communications Networks and Services Agency

156. The main regulatory body regarding broadcasting media is *Communications Networks and Services Agency (AKOS)*, which is responsible for the implementation of the ECA. AKOS's mission is to *regulate the electronic communications market* in order to ensure competitiveness, and thus make it possible to choose high-quality, modern and affordable services.

157. Agency changed its name in January 2014 (previously, Post and Communications Agency (APEK)); the *AKOS* continues to be an independent body that:

- regulates and supervises the electronic communications market;
- manages and supervises the radio frequency spectrum in the Republic of Slovenia;
- performs tasks in the field of radio and television broadcasting; and
- regulates and supervises the postal and railway service markets.

158. According to Article 251 of the ECA, the previous Post and Electronic Communications Agency of the Republic of Slovenia, which operated pursuant to the previous ECA,[71] since the implementation of the new ECA in 2012 continues its work as the *AKOS of the Republic of Slovenia* (or the Agency). The Agency has ex officio reviewed the decisions on allocating radio frequencies, issued pursuant to the previous ECA in terms of their compliance with the provisions on technological and service neutrality in Articles 28 and 29 of the ECA.

159. The Agency is a legal entity of public law; it is independent in exercising the functions that lie within its sphere of competence. The Agency exercises the rights and discharges the obligations of the founder (Government of Slovenia).

71. Official Gazette of the RS, 13/07 – official consolidated version, 102/07 – ZDRad, 110/09, 33/2011, hereinafter: Electronic Communications Act.

According to Article 192 of the ECA, judicial protection may be claimed against a final decision or other individual Agency act in accordance with the act governing administrative disputes. An administrative suit may be filed against acts issued by the Agency under this Act at the Administrative Court of the RS in Ljubljana.

C. The transition of the Electronic Communications Control from the Inspectorate to the Agency

160. According to the ECA – 1 (ZEKom-1, Official Gazette of the Republic of Slovenia No. 109/12 on 31 December 2012), the tasks and responsibilities of the former Inspectorate of the RS for Electronic Communications and Electronic Signature were moved to the AKOS. The tasks of the Inspectorate of the Republic of Slovenia for Electronic Communications and Electronic Signature were to *supervise the implementation of legislation* governing electronic communications and electronic signatures.

161. Article 254 of ECA-1 provided that within three months, the Agency shall assume the civil servants of the Inspectorate for Electronic Communications and electronic signing in the field of electronic communications to work as authorized persons of the Agency, including funds for work, rights and obligations, uncompleted cases and archives. According to Article 255 of the ECA-1 that regulates the transition from Inspectorate to Agency, public officials from the Inspectorate for Electronic Communications and Electronic Signatures engaged in the area of electronic communications moved to the Agency to work as authorized persons of the Agency.

162. The AKOS took over all the tasks and responsibilities of the former Inspectorate for Electronic Communications and Electronic Signatures, supervised since the day of the implementation of ECA-1.

II. Technological and Economic Developments on the Media Markets

A. Digital Television

163. Digital television (DTV) is the transmission of audio and video by digitally processed and multiplexed signal, in contrast to the totally analogue and channel separated signals used by analogue television. It is an innovative service that represents a significant evolution in television technology since colour television in the 1950s.[72] Conditions for implementing digital broadcasting in Slovenia, rights and obligations of providers and radio frequency spectrum management are set out by DBA.

72. Kruger, L. G. (2001). Digital Television: An Overview. Hauppauge, New York: Nova Publishers.

164. DBA also defines digital broadcasting in the Republic of Slovenia, and the gradual transition from analogue to digital broadcasting. DBA regulates inclusion and introduction of complementary and innovative services, and the gradual phasing out of analogue broadcasting The Act also sets out incentive measures for facilitating the transition to digital broadcasting.

165. Digital broadcasting was introduced in Slovenia, in accordance with the relevant EU legislation:

- *Directive 2002/20* / EC of the European Parliament and of the Council of 7 March 2002 on the *authorization of electronic communications networks and services* (*Authorization Directive*) (OJ L 108, 24.4.2002, p. 21);
- *Directive 2009/140* / EC of the European Parliament and of the Council of 25 November 2009 amending Directives 2002/21 / EC on a *common regulatory framework* for electronic communications networks and services, 2002/19 / EC on access to electronic communications networks and associated facilities and on their interconnection and 2002/20 / EC on the authorization of electronic communications networks and services (OJ L No. 337 of 18.12.2009, p. 37);
- *Directive 2002/21* / EC of the European Parliament and of the Council of 7 March 2002 on a *common regulatory framework* for electronic communications networks and services (*Framework Directive*) (OJ L 108, 24.4.2002, p. 33), last amended by Regulation (EC) No. 544/2009 of the European Parliament and of the Council of 18 June 2009 amending Regulation (EC) No. 717/2007 on roaming on public mobile telephone networks within the Community and Directive 2002/21 / EC on a common regulatory framework for electronic communications networks and services (OJ L No. 167 of 29.6.2009, p. 12);
- *Commission Directive 2002/77* / EC of 16 September 2002 on *competition in the markets* for electronic communications networks and services (OJ L No 249 of 17.9.2002, p. 21);
- *Directive 2002/20/EC* of the European Parliament and of the Council of 7 March 2002 on the *authorization of electronic communications networks and services* (OJ L 108, 24 April 2002, p. 21);

  Directive 2002/21/EC of the European Parliament and of the Council of 7 March 2002 on a *common regulatory framework for electronic communications* networks and services (OJ L 108, 24 April 2002, p. 33); and

  Commission Directive 2002/77/EC of 16 September on *competition in the markets for electronic communications* networks and services (OJ L 249, 17 September 2002, p. 21).

166. On 16 February 2006, the Government of the Republic of Slovenia adopted the *strategy of the Republic of Slovenia for the switchover from analogue to digital* broadcasting. More than two years after the adoption of the strategy, adoption and entry into force of the DBA.

167. DBA (Article 3, see also Article 27) also defines and regulates *multiplexing* as a part of a digital telecommunications broadcasting system for handling multiple digital input channels and transmitting them together.

168. DBA (Articles 29–32) sets out the rules related to the process of *transition from analogue to digital broadcasting (2009 at the latest) including the phase of* concurrent analogue and digital broadcasting. A period of concurrent analogue and digital broadcasting for all television content providers started when the coverage of the population with the signal of at least one multiplex system in a single geographical area was at least 90%. Additional condition was that all content providers with the right to disseminate programming using digital broadcasting technology in this geographical area were granted the technical option and right to transmit and disseminate programmes in the multiplex system.

169. On the day of termination of analogue television in the respective geographical area, the cessation of decisions on the assignment of radio frequencies for analogue television took place by the declaratory decision of the Agency revoking all decisions on the assignment of radio frequencies for analogue television (see also Article 31a of the DBA).

B. New Media

1. On-Demand Audio-Visual Media Services

170. On-demand audio-visual media services are *non-linear audio-visual media services* providing audio-visual content from a catalogue that is designed by the provider, while users can consume this content when they decide to. Since the adoption of the Act on Audio-Visual Media Services (November 2011) non-linear audio-visual media services expanded substantially. Unlike with traditional television, the viewer has a significantly greater range of choice when selecting and controlling the content, as well as the time they consume it.

171. The Agency is competent for administering the official record of providers of on -demand audio-visual services. A provider of on -demand audio-visual media services must declare this service to the Agency. Agency performs inspection-supervision of programming content and adhering to the rules on advertising (such as for example, sponsorships and product placement), and care for the protection of children from harmful content.[73]

172. The Act on Audio-Visual Media Services (AVMSA) imposes certain obligations on providers of on -demand audio-visual media services, and the Agency supervises their execution during inspection supervision.

73. *See also*: General Act on Declaring On Demand Audio-visual Media Services and established an official record of providers of on demand audio-visual services, enacted and published by the Agency: http://www.akos-rs.si/akos-ang.

C. The Convergence of Media Products

173. Due to the progress of technology, various different types of media (computer, television, radio and newspaper) are more developing *converged media products* and offer them to the market. Smart TV sets combine television and computer technology; websites are more and more using video technology.

174. Computers and network technology developed video services *on demand.* The internet has become important for newspaper publishers; a lot of newspapers have started to concentrate on producing websites for newspaper readers. The mobile technology attempts to deliver more and more of these services to mobile devices.

175. According to Slovenian media analysts, the future of convergence in Slovenia will probably belong to *mobile telecommunication* providers: they hold almost half of the market revenues, three quarters of all Slovenian citizens own a mobile telephone – the first electronic medium – after television – which has successfully overcome the majority of demographic factors (age, gender, education, income).[74]

176. Moreover, the mentioned media companies also offer online news and other content for mobile telephone subscribers. The two largest mobile telecommunications operators, Telekom and Si.Mobil have recently widened their offer of digital content (news, entertainment, interactive games etc.) on their platforms Planet and Vodafone live. Public service broadcaster RTV Slovenia and the biggest commercial broadcaster Pro Plus offer a wide variety of content.[75]

177. Despite progress in recent years, the state of convergence in Slovenia is *still at the outset.* The main pillars of convergence have been built on four interconnected levels: a technological level (mainly due to digitalizing of broadcasting, IT and telecommunications networks), a structural level (as a consequence of corporate alliances across different sectors), a content level (more profound, broad and easily accessible content), and a market level (as a response to convergence on first three levels).[76]

D. Film and Audio-Visual Industry

178. The National Programme for Culture 2014 – 2017, among others, envisages measures for the *development of the cinematographic and audio-visual sectors*; the fact is that in the past all aspects of the cinematographic production chain were neglected due to the insufficient public support for the film and audio-visual

74. Igor Vobič, Faculty of Social Sciences, University of Ljubljana, Slovenia, Marko Milosavljević Faculty of Social Sciences, University of Ljubljana Slovenia, Media Landscape of Slovenia.
75. *Ibid.*
76. *Ibid.*

industry. The measures are intended to increase the number of viewers and to increase the market for cinematographic and audio-visual production, to develop the cinematographic network and support for film culture programmes, to enhance the use of digital technologies.

179. The crucial feature of the policy is a new financing scheme introducing non-budget funds in the form of contributions to be paid by all participants in the cinematographic chain as a percentage of annual gross income from services provided; these participants will be represented on the council of Slovenia's Film Centre and will thus be able to participate in shaping a comprehensive film policy[77]

§4. Sources of Media Law

I. Legislation: Slovenia

A. Constitution of the Republic of Slovenia

180. Constitution of the Republic of Slovenia (CS), Official Gazette U33/1991 as of 28. 12. 1991 stipulates freedoms and rights of citizens, including those, of major direct relevance for the media law in Slovenia. Of direct media relevances are the *freedom of expression* and the *right to correction and reply.*

181. But there are other fundamental rights that form the Constitutional framework for a democratic and open society, such as:

- *Equality before the Law* (Article 14 of the Constitution of Slovenia, hereinafter CS);
- *Protection of Human Personality and Dignity* (Article 21 of the CS);
- *Equal Protection of Rights* (Article 22 of the CS);
- *Public Nature of Court Proceedings* (Article 24 of the CS);
- *Presumption of Innocence (*Article 27 of the CS);
- *Right to Personal Dignity and Safety* (Article 34 of the CS);
- *Protection of Right to Privacy and Personality Rights* (Article 35 of the CS);
- *Protection of the Privacy of Correspondence and Other Means of Communication* (Article 37 of the CS);
- *Protection of Personal Data (*Article 38 of the CS);
- *Freedom of Conscience (*Article 41 of the CS);
- *Participation in the Management of Public Affairs* (Article 44 of the CS);
- *Prohibition of Incitement to Discrimination and Intolerance* and *Prohibition of Incitement to Violence and War* (Article 63).

77. The National Program for Culture 2014 – 2017, adopted in 2013 by the National Assembly at the proposal of the government, contains development goals and measures to unlock development potential in different areas, and establish culture as an essential factor of development of both the individual and society.

182. As for *freedom of expression,* Article 39 of the Constitution of Slovenia stipulates as one of the fundamental Constitutional freedoms. Freedom of expression encompasses freedom of thought, freedom of speech and freedom of public appearance. Freedom of expression further on includes freedom of the press and other forms of public communication and expression. According to the Constitution of Slovenia freedom of expression shall be guaranteed.

183. Constitution of Slovenia guarantees everyone to freely collect, receive and disseminate information and opinions. Except in such cases, as are provided by law, everyone has the right to obtain information of a public nature in which he/she has a well-founded legal interest under the law (Article 39 of the Constitution of Slovenia).

184. The right to correct published information which has damaged a right or interest of an individual, organization or body is guaranteed, as it is the right to reply to such published information (Article 40 of the Constitution of Slovenia).Both rights (*Correction and Reply*) are in details elaborated in the respective Law on Mass Media.

B. Legislation

The Mass Media Act

185. The MMA (Official Gazette of the Republic of Slovenia, No. 110/06 – official consolidated text, 36/08 – ZPOmK-1, 77/10 – ZSFCJA, 90/10 – Rev. US, 87/11 – ZAvMS, 47/12, 47/15 – ZZSDT, 22/16 and 39/16) was enacted back in 2001 and amended since then several times.

The unofficial consolidated text of the MMA[78] includes: Media Act – ZMed (Official Gazette of the Republic of Slovenia, No. 35/01 of 11.5.2001), stipulates the rights, obligations and responsibilities of legal and natural persons and the public interest in the area of the mass media. It includes numerous amendments:

- MMA – ZMed (Official Gazette of the Republic of Slovenia, No. 35/01 of 11.5.2001);
- Decision to repeal Article 107 of the Media Act (Official Gazette of the Republic of Slovenia, No. 113/03 of 20.11.2003);
- Decision on the partial annulment of Article 82 of the Media Act and repealing the Rules on criteria for financing programming content of radio or television programmes with status of local, regional and student significance (Official Gazette of the Republic of Slovenia, No. 16/04 of 20 February 2004);
- Decision annulling the sixth and seventh paragraphs of Article 112 of the Media Act (Official Gazette of the Republic of Slovenia, No. 123/04 of 18.11.2004);

78. http://pisrs.si/Pis.web/pregledPredpisa?id=ZAKO1608: English translation of MMA: https://www.rtvslo.si/files/razno/mass_media_act.pdf.

- Radio -Television Slovenia Act – ZRTVS-1 (Official Gazette of the Republic of Slovenia, No. 96/05 of 28.10.2005);
- Amending the Media Act – ZMed-A (Official Gazette of the Republic of Slovenia, No. 60/06 of 9 June 2006);
- Compulsory copy of publications – ZOIPub (Official Gazette of the Republic of Slovenia, No. 69/06 of 3 July 2006);
- Media Act – official consolidated text – ZMed-UPB1 (Official Gazette of the Republic of Slovenia, No. 110/06 of 26.10.2006);
- Prevention of Restriction of Competition Act – ZPOmK-1 (Official Gazette of the Republic of Slovenia, No. 36/08 of 11.4.2008);
- Act on the Slovenian Film Center, the Public Agency of the Republic of Slovenia – ZSFCJA (Official Gazette of the Republic of Slovenia, No. 77/10 of 4 October 2010);
- Decision on the finding that the second paragraph of Article 26 of the Media Act is inconsistent with the Constitution and the annulment of the judgment of the Supreme Court, the judgment of the Higher Court in Koper and the judgment of the District Court in Koper (Official Gazette of the Republic of Slovenia, No. 90/10 of 12. 11. 2010);
- Audio-visual Media Services Act – ZAvMS (Official Gazette of the Republic of Slovenia, No. 87/11 of 2 November 2011);
- Act Amending the Media Act – ZMed-B (Official Gazette of the Republic of Slovenia, No. 47/12 of 22 June 2012);
- Employment, Self-Employment and Work of Aliens Act – ZZSDT (Official Gazette of the Republic of Slovenia, No. 47/15 of 30 June 2015);
- Act Amending the Media Act – ZMed-C (Official Gazette of the Republic of Slovenia, No. 22/16 of 25.3.2016);
- Act Amending the Media Act – ZMed-D (Official Gazette of the Republic of Slovenia, No. 39/16 of 3 June 2016.

Mass media, under the MMA, are newspapers and magazines, radio and television programme services, electronic publications, teletext and other forms of the editorially formulated programme published daily or periodically through the transmission of written material, vocal material, sound or pictures in a manner accessible to the public. The term 'mass media' does not cover bulletins, catalogues, other forms of publication of information intended exclusively for advertising, business communication, educational processes or the internal work of companies, institutions and foundations, societies, political parties, and church and other organizations, school gazettes, the Official Gazette of the Republic of Slovenia and the official gazettes of local communities, other official publications, posters, pamphlets, brochures and transparencies, and video pages without moving pictures (unpaid reports), unless stipulated otherwise by law.

Act on RTV (ARTV)

186. Act on Radio and Television, ARTV (Official Gazette of the Republic of Slovenia, No. 96/05, 109/05 – ZDavP-1B, 105/06 – Rev. US, 26/09 – ZIPRS0809-B and 9/14, Slov.: Zakon o Radioteleviziji Slovenija, ZRTVS-1) was enacted in 2005, and since then, it has been amended several times.

The unofficial consolidated text No. 4 of the ARTE includes the following changes:

- Radio Television Slovenia Act – ZRTVS-1 (Official Gazette of the Republic of Slovenia, No. 96/05 of 28.10.2005);
- Act Amending the Tax Procedure Act – ZDavP-1B (Official Gazette RS, No. 109/05 of 6 December 2005);
- Decision to annul the second paragraph of Article 15 of the Radiotelevizija Slovenija Act (Official Gazette of the Republic of Slovenia, No. 105/06 of 12.10.2006);
- Act Amending the Implementation of the Budget of the Republic of Slovenia for the years 2008 and 2009 – ZIPRS0809-B (Official Gazette of the Republic of Slovenia, No. 26/09 of 6 April 2009);
- Act Amending the Radiotelevizija Slovenija Act – ZRTVS-1A (Official Gazette of the Republic of Slovenia, No. 9/14 of 5 February 2014).ARTV.

ARTE regulates the *status and operation of the Radio and Television* Corporation of Slovenia (hereinafter *RTV* Slovenia). RTV Slovenia is an independent legal person of special cultural and national importance governed by public law. Within the performance of public service laid down by the Act, RTV Slovenia provides a wide range of contents, programmes and services, without discrimination and on the basis of equal opportunities, through various transmission paths.

Slovenian Press Agency Act

187. Slovenian Press Agency Act (SPAA – Official Gazette RS, No. 50/11, Slov.: Zakon o slovenski tiskovni agenciji, ZSTA) regulates the status and functioning of the Slovenian Press Agency (hereinafter referred to as STA). STA performs a public service permanent, comprehensive, accurate and objective provision of information about events in Slovenia and around the world to meet the needs of the public in the Republic of Slovenia and Slovenians abroad and Slovenian minorities in neighbouring countries in the Slovenian language as well as on developments in Slovenia for the needs of the media and the public in the Republic of Slovenia and outside the borders of the Republic of Slovenia in the English language in accordance with this act, establishing the STA and the law regulating the media.

188. STA is organized as a limited liability company. For issues not regulated by the SPAA, the law governing commercial companies applies. STA is the issuer of the medium in accordance with the law that governs media. The sole founder and partner of the STA is the Republic of Slovenia. STA performs a public service every day by creation, preparation, preservation and dissemination of news abstracts containing the key, the most essential information about the event, the developments in Slovenia and around the world in Slovenian and English in the following areas;

politics, economy, culture, education, health, chronicle, sport, events from the world, science, voluntary work and non-governmental organizations, entertainment and other content.

Act on Audio-Visual Media Services

189. *AVMSA*[79] Official Gazette No. 87/2011 of 19 October 2011, Slov.: Zakon o avdiovizualnih medijskih storitvah, ZAMS) stipulates, that audio-visual media service consists of service provision of audio-visual broadcasts, carried out an economic activity, including the activity of public service enterprises, and is under the editorial responsibility of the audio-visual media service provider and through electronic communications networks to the general public in the form of linear or non-linear audio-visual media services in order to information, entertainment or education, or audio-visual commercial communication.

The AVMSA was once substantially amended in 2015. The unofficial consolidated text of the Audio-visual Media Services Act includes:

- Audio-visual Media Services Act – ZAvMS (Official Gazette of the Republic of Slovenia, No. 87/11 of 2 November 2011);
- Act Amending and Supplementing the Audio-visual Media Services Act – ZAvMS-A (Official Gazette RS, No. 84/15 of 6 November 2015).

With this Act, the Directive 2010/13/EU of the European Parliament and of the Council of 10 March 2010 on the coordination of certain provisions laid down by law, regulation or administrative action in Member States concerning the provision of audio-visual media services (Audio-visual Media Services Directive) (codified version) (OJ L 95 of 15.4.2010) (hereinafter: Directive 2010/13 / EU) is brought to legal order of the RS.

190. The audio-visual media services may be covered so text-based content, which accompanies audio-visual broadcasts, for example, captions or electronic programme guides. From the audio-visual media service are excluded services whose principal purpose is the provision of audio-visual broadcasting. When the service audio-visual elements are present merely incidental to the service only, such as website with animated elements, short advertising spots or information related to a product or service that does not fall within the scope of audio-visual media services, stand-alone text-based services, electronic versions of newspapers and magazines, gambling of money, lotteries, betting and other forms of gambling services in the field, online games, and web search engines.

Electronic Communications Act

---

79. http://www.uradni-list.si/1/objava.jsp?urlid=201187&stevilka=3715; www.en.uni.lu/content/download/46784/536648/file/Slovenia_translation.pdf [unofficial English translation].

191. ECA (Official Gazette of the Republic of Slovenia, Nos 109/12, 110/13, 40/14 – ZIN-B, 54/14 – Rev. US, 81/15 and 40/17 Zakon o elektronskih komunikacijah, ZEKom) enacted in 2004 was last amended in 2017.

The unofficial, consolidated text of the ECA comprises a number of changes, as follows:

- Electronic Communications Act – ZEKom-1 (Official Gazette of the Republic of Slovenia, No. 109/12 of 31.12.2012);
- Act Amending and Supplementing the Electronic Communications Act – ZEKom-1A (Official Gazette of the Republic of Slovenia, No. 110/13 of 27 December 2013);
- Act Amending the Inspection Supervision Act – ZIN-B (Official Gazette of the Republic of Slovenia, No. 40/14 of 3 June 2014);
- Decision to repeal Articles 162, 163, 164, 165, 166, 167, 168 and 169 of the Electronic Communications Act (Official Gazette of the Republic of Slovenia, No. 54/14 of 18.7.2014);
- Act Amending the Electronic Communications Act – ZEKom-1B (Official Gazette of the Republic of Slovenia, No. 81/15 of 30.10.2015);
- Act Amending the Electronic Communications Act – ZEKom-1C (Official Gazette of the Republic of Slovenia, No. 40/17 of 21.7.2017).

ECA regulates the conditions for the provision of electronic communications networks and implementation of electronic communications services as universal service. The Act ensures competition and management of the radio frequency spectrum and numbering resources, determines the conditions for restriction of property rights, provides for the rights of users, regulating the safety of networks and services and their performance in exceptional situations, providing exercise and regulating the protection of the right to communication privacy of users of public communications services shall be governed by the settlement of disputes between operators in the electronic communications market. The Act regulates competence, organization and functioning of the Agency for electronic communications networks and services of the Republic of Slovenia as an independent regulatory authority and powers of other bodies carrying out functions under this Act, and other issues related to electronic communications.

The Electronic Commerce and Electronic Signature Act (ECESA)

192. ECESA (Official Gazette of the Republic of Slovenia, No. 98/04 – official consolidated text, 61/06 – ZEPT and 46/14). *ECESA* Slovene: Zakon o elektronskem poslovanju in elektronskem podpisu – ZEPEP (regulates *electronic commerce*, which includes *operations in electronic form* through the use of information and communication technologies and the use of electronic signatures in legal transactions, including e-commerce in judicial, administrative and other similar procedures, unless the law provides otherwise.

The unofficial consolidated text of the ECESA comprises the following changes:

- Electronic Commerce and Electronic Signature Act – ZEPEP (Official Gazette of the Republic of Slovenia, No. 57/00 of 23 June 2000);
- Act Amending the Act on the Organization and Work of the Ministries – ZODPM-C (Official Gazette of the Republic of Slovenia, No. 30/01 of 26.4.2001);
- Act Amending the Electronic Commerce and Electronic Signature Act – ZEPEP-A (Official Gazette of the Republic of Slovenia, No. 25/04 of 19 March 2004);
- Act Amending the Law on Notaries – ZN-C (Official Gazette of the Republic of Slovenia, No. 73/04 of 5 July 2004);
- Electronic Commerce and Electronic Signature Act – official consolidated text – ZEPEP-UPB1 (Official Gazette of the Republic of Slovenia, No. 98/04 of 9 September 2004);
- Electronic Commerce Act on the Market – ZEPT (Official Gazette of the Republic of Slovenia, No. 61/06 of 13.6.2006);
- Act Amending and Supplementing the Electronic Commerce and Electronic Signature Act – ZEPEP-B (Official Gazette of the Republic of Slovenia, No. 46/14 of 23 June 2014.

Digital Broadcasting Act

193. The DBA (Official Gazette of the Republic of Slovenia, Nos 102/07, 85/10, 47/12 and 109/12 – ZEKom-1). Slov.: Zakon o digitalni radiodifuziji, ZDRa, defines digital broadcasting in the Republic of Slovenia, sets out conditions for implementing digital broadcasting, rights and obligations of providers, changes in radio frequency spectrum management, the gradual transition from analogue to digital broadcasting, inclusion and introduction of complementary and innovative services, and the gradual phasing out of analogue broadcasting and incentive measures for facilitating the transition to digital broadcasting.

The unofficial consolidated text of the DBA encompasses:

- Digital Broadcasting Act – ZDRad (Official Gazette of the Republic of Slovenia, No. 102/07 of 9.11.2007);
- Act Amending the Digital Broadcasting Act – ZDRad-A (Official Gazette of the Republic of Slovenia, No. 85/10 of 29.10.2010);
- Act Amending the Digital Broadcasting Act – ZDRad-B (Official Gazette of the Republic of Slovenia, No. 47/12 of 22 June 2012);
- Electronic Communications Act – ZEKom-1 (Official Gazette of the Republic of Slovenia, No. 109/12 of 31.12.2012).

Personal Data Protection Act

194. Personal Data Protection Act (PDPA)[1] Official Gazette of the Republic of Slovenia, No. 86/2004, as of 5 August 2004, as amended by 113/2005-ZInfP, 51/2007-ZUstS-A, 67/2007, 94/2007-UPB1 (official consolidated text) (Slov.:

Zakon o varstvu osebnih podatkov, ZVOP-1) determines the rights, responsibilities, principles and measures to prevent unconstitutional, unlawful and unjustified encroachments on the privacy and dignity of an individual in the processing of personal data. According to the PDPA-1, personal data must be processed lawfully and fairly. PDPA-1 applies to the processing of personal data if the data controller or if a subsidiary of the data controller is registered in the Republic of Slovenia.

The unofficial consolidated text of the law on the protection of personal data comprises the changes, as follows:

- The law on the protection of personal data-ZVOP-1 (Official Journal of the Republic of Slovenia, No. 86/04 of 5 November 1999);
- The Information Proxy Act-ZInfP (Official Journal of the Republic of Slovenia, No 113/05 of 16 June 1999);
- Law on amendments and additions to the law on the Constitutional Court-ZUstS-A (Official Journal of the Republic of Slovenia, No. 51/07 of 8 June 1993);
- Act on amendments and additions to the law on the protection of personal data-ZVOP-1a (Official Journal of the Republic of Slovenia, No. 67/07 of 27 June 1993);
- The law on the protection of personal data-officially consolidated text-ZVOP-1-UPB1 (Official Journal of the Republic of Slovenia, No. 94/07 of 16 June 1993);

Access to Public Information Act

195. Access to Public Information Act (APIA), official consolidated version (Slov.: Zakon o dostopu do informacij javnega značaja, ZDIJZ, UPB2, Official Gazette of the Republic of Slovenia, No. 51/06) governs the procedure which everyone free access to and reuse of public information held by state bodies, local government bodies, public agencies, public funds and other entities of public law, public powers holders and public service contractors.

The unofficial consolidated text of the law on access to public-character information comprises the following changes:

- The law on access to public information – ZDIJZ (Official Journal of the Republic of Slovenia, No. 24/03 of 7 March 2001);
- The law on amendments and additions to the law on access to public information – ZDIJZ-A (Official Journal of the Republic of Slovenia No. 61/05 of June 2005);
- The law on access to public information, officially consolidated text – ZDIJZ-UPB1 (Official Journal of the Republic of Slovenia, No. 96/05 of 28 March 1994);
- The law on amendments and additions to the law on tax procedure – ZDavP-1b (Official Journal of the Republic of Slovenia, No. 109/05 of 6 July 1994);
- The Information Proxy Act – ZInfP (Official Journal of the Republic of Slovenia, No. 113/05 of 16 June 1999);

– The law on amendments and additions to the law on access to public information – ZDIJZ-B (Official Journal of the Republic of Slovenia, No. 28/06 of 17 June 1993);
– The law on access to public information, officially consolidated text – ZDIJZ-UPB2 (Official Journal of the Republic of Slovenia, No. 51/06 of 3 May 2006).

Penal Code

196. Penal Code (PC), Official Gazette No. 63/1994 (70/1994), No. 23/1999, 60/1999 Odl.US: U-I-226/95, 110/2002-ZDT-B, 40/2004, 95/2004-UPB1, 37/2005 Odl.US: U-I-335/02-20, 17/2006 Odl.US: U-I-192/04-16, 55/2008-KZ-1 (66/2008 popr.), 89/2008 Odl.US: U-I-25/07-43, *PC* (Official Journal of the Republic of Slovenia, No. 50/12 – officially consolidated text, 6/16 – Popr, 54/15, 38/16 and 27/17), Slovene: Kazenski zakonik, KZ in the chapter, titled: Criminal Offences Against Honour and Reputation, incriminates the following criminal actions, that can also be done by press or broadcasting: insult, defamation, injurious accusation, exposure of personal and family circumstances, reproaching of a criminal offence with the intention to disparage (Articles 158–162). All these criminal actions can be done by press or broadcasting as a qualified manner.

The unofficial consolidated text of the PC comprises several changes, as follows:

– Criminal Code – KZ-1 (Official Journal of the Republic of Slovenia, No. 55/08 of 4 November 1993. 6.2008);
– Correction of the Criminal Code – KZ-1 (Official Journal of the Republic of Slovenia, No. 66/08 of 1 January 2003, 7.2008);
– Act Amending the Penal Code – KZ-1a (Official Journal of the Republic of Slovenia, No. 39/09 of 26 July 1991. 5.2009);
– The law on amendments and additions to the Penal Code – KZ-1b (Official Journal of the Republic of Slovenia, No. 91/11 of 14 November 1993, 11.2011);
– Penal Code – officially consolidated text – KZ-1-UPB2 (Official Journal of the Republic of Slovenia, No. 50/12 of 29 June 1993. 6.2012);
– Correction of the official consolidated text of the Criminal Code – KZ-1-UPB2p (Official Journal of the Republic of Slovenia, No. 6/16 of 29 November 1999. 1.2016);
– The law on amendments and additions to the Penal Code – KZ-1c (Official Journal of the Republic of Slovenia, No. 54/15 of 20 November 1999, 7.2015);
– Act Amending the Penal Code – KZ-1d (Official Journal of the Republic of Slovenia, No. 38/16 of 27 June 1993. 5.2016);
– The law on amendments and additions to the Penal Code – KZ-1E (Official Journal of the Republic of Slovenia, No. 27/17 of 2 July 2003. 6.2017);

Code of Obligations (CO)

197. Code of Obligations, (Official Journal of the Republic of Slovenia, No. 97/07 – officially consolidated text, 64/16 – ODL. US and 20/18 – OROZ631) sets out legal basis for damage liability with the general provision, that any person that inflicts damage on another shall be obliged to reimburse it, unless it is proved that the damage was incurred without the culpability of the former. Obligations Code in Article 132 defines the expression 'damage'; it stipulates, that damage comprises the diminution of property (ordinary damage), prevention of the appreciation of property (lost profits), the infliction of physical or mental distress or fear on another person, and encroachment upon the reputation of a legal person. Damage can though be material or/and immaterial. OZ-UPB1 regulates also reimbursement of material damage in case of defamation or calumny.

The unofficial consolidated text of the Obligatory Code includes some changes:

- Obligatory Code – OZ (Official Gazette RS, No. 83/01 of 25.10.2001);
- Decision on the partial annulment of Article 1060 of the Obligatory Code (Official Gazette of the Republic of Slovenia, No. 28/06 of 17.3.2006);
- Act Amending and Supplementing the Obligatory Code – OZ-A (Official Gazette of the Republic of Slovenia, No. 40/07 of 7.5.2007);
- Obligatory Code – official consolidated text – OZ-UPB1 (Official Gazette of the Republic of Slovenia, No. 97/07 of 24.10.2007);
- Decision to repeal Article 184 of the Code of Obligations (Official Gazette of the Republic of Slovenia, No. 64/16 of 14.10.2016);

C. Other Legislation, Related to Media

198. Following are listed pieces of legislation, which are indirectly rather than directly important and relevant for media:

- *General Administrative Procedure Act* (Official Gazette RS, No. 24/2006, 105/2006-ZUS-1, 126/2007, 65/2008,47/2009 Odl.US: U-I-54/06-32 (48/2009 corr.) in 8/2010);
- *Inspection Act* – (Official Gazette RS, No. 43/2007-UPB1);
- *Minor Offences Act* (Official Gazette RS, No. 29/2011-UPB8, 43/2011 Odl. US: U-I-166/10-8);
- *Administrative Dispute Act* (Official Gazette RS, No. 105/2006, 26/2007 Skl.US: U-I-69/07-9, 122/2007 Skl.US: U-I-264/05-23, U-I-181/07, Up-2126/07-10, 65/2008 Odl.US: U-I-98/07-27, 119/2008 Odl.US: U-I-69/07-36, 54/2009 Odl.US: Up-1782/08-16, U-I-166/08-8, 107/2009 Odl.US: U-I-147/08-16, Up-1547/08-17, 14/2010 Odl.US: U-I-303/08-9, 62/2010, 14/2011 Skl.US: U-I-55/09-8, Up-257/09-10, 93/2011 Odl.US: U-I-16/10-10, Up-103/10-12, 98/2011 Odl.US: U-I-181/09-15, Up-860/09-14, Up-222/10-14);
- *Information Commissioner Act* (Official Gazette of the Republic of Slovenia, No. 113/05 and 51/07 – ZUstS-A).

The unofficial consolidated text of the Information Commissioner Act includes:

- *Act on Information Commissioner – ZInfP* (Official Gazette of the Republic of Slovenia, No. 113/05 of 16.12.2005);

- *Act Amending the Constitutional Court Act – ZUstS-A* (Official Gazette of the Republic of Slovenia, No. 51/07 of 8 June 2007);
- *Public Agencies Act* (Official Gazette RS, No. 52/2002, 51/2004-EZ-A, 33/2011-ZEKom-C);
- *State Administration Act* (Official Gazette of the Republic of Slovenia, No. 113/05 – official consolidated text, 89/07 – decree US, 126/07 – ZUP-E, 48/09, 8/10 – ZUP-G, 8/12 – ZVRS-F, 21/12, 47/13, 12/14, 90/14 and 51/16).

The unofficial consolidated text of the State Administration Act comprises numerous changes that constantly take place:

- State Administration Act – ZDU-1 (Official Gazette of the Republic of Slovenia, No. 52/02 of 14.6.2002);
- Act Amending the Law on State Administration – ZDU-1A (Official Gazette of the Republic of Slovenia, No. 56/03 of 13.6.2003);
- State Administration Act – official consolidated text – ZDU-1-UPB1 (Official Gazette of the Republic of Slovenia, No. 83/03 of 22.8.2003);
- Act Amending the State Administration Act – ZDU-1B (Official Gazette of the Republic of Slovenia, No. 61/04 of 4.6.2004),– State Administration Act – official consolidated text – ZDU-1-UPB2 (Official Gazette of the Republic of Slovenia, No. 97/04 of 3 September 2004);
- Act Amending the State Administration Act – ZDU-1C (Official Gazette of the Republic of Slovenia, No. 123/04 of 18.11.2004);
- State Administration Act – official consolidated text;
- ZDU-1-UPB3 (Official Gazette of the Republic of Slovenia, No. 24/05 of 11.3.2005);
- Act Amending the State Administration Act – ZDU-1D (Official Gazette of the Republic of Slovenia, No. 93/05 of 21.10.2005);
- State Administration Act – official consolidated text – ZDU-1-UPB4 (Official Gazette of the Republic of Slovenia, No. 113/05 of 16.12.2005);
- Decision on the annulment of Article 2 of the Act Amending the Act on State Administration (Official Gazette of the Republic of Slovenia, No. 89/07 of 2.10.2007);
- Act Amending and Supplementing the General Administrative Procedure Act – ZUP-E (Official Gazette of the Republic of Slovenia, No. 126/07 of 31.12.2007);
- Act Amending the State Administration Act – ZDU-1E (Official Gazette of the Republic of Slovenia, No. 48/09 of 26.6.2009);
- Act Amending the General Administrative Procedure Act – ZUP-G (Official Gazette of the Republic of Slovenia, No. 8/10 of 5 February 2010);
- Act Amending the Act on the Government of the Republic of Slovenia – ZVRS-F (Official Gazette of the Republic of Slovenia, No. 8/12 of 3 February 2012);
- Act Amending the State Administration Act – ZDU-1F (Official Gazette of the Republic of Slovenia, No. 21/12 of 19 March 2012;
- Act Amending the State Administration Act – ZDU-1G (Official Gazette of the Republic of Slovenia, No. 47/13 of 31 May 2013);
- Act Amending the State Administration Act – ZDU-1H (Official Gazette of the Republic of Slovenia, No. 12/14 of 14.2.2014);

– Act Amending the State Administration Act – ZDU-1I (Official Gazette of the Republic of Slovenia, No. 90/14 of 15.12.2014);
– Act Amending the State Administration Act – ZDU-1J (Official Gazette of the Republic of Slovenia, No. 51/16 of 22 July 2016).

Civil Servants Act (Official Gazette of the Republic of Slovenia, No. 63/07 – official consolidated text, 65/08, 69/08 – ZTFI-A, 69/08 – ZZavar-E and 40/12 – ZUJF)

The unofficial consolidated text of the Civil Servants Act includes the following changes:

– The Law on Civil Servants – ZJU (Official Gazette RS, No. 56/02 of 28 June 2002);
– Act Amending the Act on the State Prosecutor's Office – ZDT-B (Official Gazette of the Republic of Slovenia, No. 110/02 of 18.12.2002);
– Labour and Social Courts Act – ZDSS-1 (Official Gazette of the Republic of Slovenia, No. 2/04 of 15 January 2004);
– Act Amending the Civil Servants Act – ZJU-A (Official Gazette of the Republic of Slovenia, No. 23/05 of 10.3.2005);
– The Law on Civil Servants – official consolidated text – ZJU-UPB1 (Official Gazette of the Republic of Slovenia, No. 35/05 of 5.4.2005);
– Decision on the partial annulment of the first paragraph of Article 193 of the Civil Servants Act (Official Gazette of the Republic of Slovenia, No. 62/05 of 1.7.2005);
– Decision on the annulment of Article 3 and finding the inconsistency of the first paragraph of Article 1 of the Act Amending the Civil Servants Act (Official Gazette of the Republic of Slovenia, No. 75/05 of 9.8. 2005);
– Act Amending and Supplementing the Civil Servants Act – ZJU-B (Official Gazette of the Republic of Slovenia, No. 113/05 of 16.12.2005);
– The Law on Civil Servants – official consolidated text – ZJU-UPB2 (Official Gazette of the Republic of Slovenia, No. 32/06 of 28.3.2006);
– Act Amending the Public Sector Salary System Act – ZSPJS-F (Official Gazette of the Republic of Slovenia, No. 68/06 of 30.6.2006);
– Decision to annul the second paragraph of Article 162 of the Civil Servants Act and Article 86 of the Act Amending the Civil Servants Act (Official Gazette of the Republic of Slovenia, No. 131/06 of 14.12.2006);
– Act Amending the Civil Servants Act – ZJU-C (Official Gazette of the Republic of Slovenia, No. 33/07 of 13.4.2007);
– Civil Servants Act – official consolidated text – ZJU-UPB3 (Official Gazette of the Republic of Slovenia, No. 63/07 of 13.7.2007);
– Act Amending and Supplementing the Civil Servants Act – ZJU-D (Official Gazette of the Republic of Slovenia, No. 65/08 of 30.6.2008);
– Act Amending the Market in Financial Instruments Act – ZTFI-A (Official Gazette of the Republic of Slovenia, No. 69/08 of 08.7.2008);
– Act Amending the Insurance Act – ZZavar-E (Official Gazette of the Republic of Slovenia, No. 69/08 of 08.072008);

– Public Finance Balance Act – ZUJF (Official Gazette of the Republic of Slovenia, No. 40/12 of 30.5.2012).

The Act on the Protection of Documentary and Archival Materials and Archives (Official Gazette of the Republic of Slovenia, No. 30/06 and 51/14), amended by the Act Amending and Supplementing the Act on the Protection of Documentary and Archival Materials and Archives – ZVDAGA-A (Official Gazette of the Republic of Slovenia, No. 51/14 of 7 July 2014).

Public Procurement Act (Official Gazette RS, Nos 128/2006, 16/2008, 19/2010, 18/2011 in 43/2012 Odl.US: U-I-211/11), amended by the Act Amending the Public Procurement Act – ZJN-2D (Official Gazette of the Republic of Slovenia, No. 90/12 of 30 November 2012), amended by:

– Public Procurement Act – official consolidated text – ZJN-2-UPB5 (Official Gazette of the Republic of Slovenia, No. 12/13 of 07.022013);
– Act Amending the Public Procurement Act – ZJN-2E (Official Gazette of the Republic of Slovenia, No. 19/14 of 17.3.2014);
– Act Amending the State Administration Act – ZDU-1I (Official Gazette of the Republic of Slovenia, No. 90/14 of 15.12.2014).

Integrity and Prevention of Corruption Act (Official Gazette of the Republic of Slovenia, No. 69/11 – official consolidated text) (69/2011-UPB2)

D. Community Legislation, Related to Broadcasting

1. EU Directives

199. Council Directive 89/552/EEC of 3 October 1989 on the coordination of certain provisions laid down by law, regulation or administrative action in Member States concerning the pursuit of television broadcasting activities (OJ L No. 298 of 17 October 1989, p. 23),

200. Directive 90/313/EEC and Directive 2003/98/EC of the European Parliament and of the Council of 17 November 2003 on the reuse of public sector information.

201. Directive 97/36/EC of the European Parliament and of the Council of 30 June 1997 amending Council Directive 89/552/EEC on the coordination of certain provisions laid down by law, regulation or administrative action in Member States concerning the pursuit of television broadcasting activities (OJ L No. 202 of 3 July 1997, p. 60).

202. Directive 2002/19/EC of the European Parliament and of the Council of 7 March 2002 on access to, and interconnection of, electronic communications networks and associated facilities (Access Directive) (OJ L 108, 24.4.2002, p. 7), as last amended by Directive 2009/140/EC of the European Parliament and of the Council of 25 November 2009 amending Directives 2002/21/EC on a common regulatory framework for electronic communications networks and services, 2002/19/EC on access to, and interconnection of, electronic communications networks and associated facilities and 2002/20/EC on the authorization of electronic communications networks and services (OJ L 337, 18.12.2009, p. 37) (hereinafter: Directive 2009/140/EC);

203. Directive 2002/20/EC of the European Parliament and of the Council of 7 March 2002 on the authorization of electronic communications networks and services (Authorization Directive) (OJ L 108, 24.4.2002, p. 21), as last amended by Directive 2009/140/EC;

204. Directive 2002/21/EC of the European Parliament and of the Council of 7 March 2002 on a common regulatory framework for electronic communications networks and services (Framework Directive) (OJ L 108, 24.4.2002, p. 33), as last amended by Directive 2009/140/EC;

205. Directive 2002/22/EC of the European Parliament and of the Council of 7 March 2002 on universal service and users' rights relating to electronic communications networks and services (Universal Service Directive) (OJ L 108, 24.4.2002, p. 51), as last amended by Directive 2009/136/EC of the European Parliament and of the Council of 25 November 2009 amending Directive 2002/22/EC on universal service and users' rights relating to electronic communications networks and services, Directive 2002/58/EC of the European Parliament and of the Council of 12 July 2002 concerning the processing of personal data and the protection of privacy in the electronic communications sector, and Regulation (EC) No 2006/2004 on cooperation between national authorities responsible for the enforcement of construction protection laws (OJ L 337, 18.12.2009, p. 11) (hereinafter: Directive 2009/136/EC);

206. Directive 2002/58/EC of the European Parliament and of the Council of 12 July 2002 concerning the processing of personal data and the protection of privacy in the electronic communications sector (Directive on privacy and electronic communications) (OJ L 201, 31.7.2002, p. 37), as last amended by Directive 2009/136/EC;

207. Commission Directive 2002/77/EC of 16 September 2002 on competition in the markets for electronic communications networks and services (OJ L 249, 17.9.2002, p. 21);

208. Directive 2010/13/EU of the European Parliament and of the council of 10 March 2010 on the coordination of certain provisions laid down by law, regulation or administrative action in Member States concerning the provision of audio-visual media services (Audio-visual Media Services Directive)

209. *Directive 2002/58/EC* of the European Parliament and of the Council of 12 July 2002 concerning the processing of personal data and the protection of privacy in the electronic communications sector (Directive on privacy and electronic communications) (OJ L 201, 31.7.2002, p. 37), as last amended by Directive 2009/136/EC;

210. *Commission Directive 2002/77/EC* of 16 September 2002 on competition in the markets for electronic communications networks and services (OJ L 249, 17.9.2002, p. 21);

211. *Directive 2006/24/EC* of the European Parliament and of the Council of 15 March 2006 on the retention of data generated or processed in connection with the provision of publicly available electronic communications services or of public communications networks and amending Directive 2002/58/EC (OJ L 106, 13.4.2006, p. 54).

212. *Directive 2007/65/EC ('Audio-visual media services without frontiers' Directive)* of the European Parliament and of the Council of 11 December 2007 amending Council Directive 89/552/EC on the coordination of certain provisions laid down by law, regulation or administrative action in Member States concerning the pursuit of television broadcasting activities. The purpose of the 'Audio-visual media services' Directive is to revise the 'Television without frontiers' (TVWF) Directive adopted in 1989 and first amended in 1997. The aim is to achieve a modern, flexible and simplified framework for audio-visual media content. The revision proposed by the Commission is based on a new definition of audio-visual media services, which is independent of the method of broadcasting.

213. *Directive 2010/13/EU (Audio-visual Media Services Directive)* of the European Parliament and of the Council of 10 March 2010 on the coordination of certain provisions laid down by law, regulation or administrative action in Member States concerning the provision of audio-visual media services (Text with EEA relevance). The Directive regulates cross-border media services and applies to media service providers when the head office of the provider and the editorial decisions taken about the audio-visual media services are located in the same or different Member States or in a third country and the service provider uses a satellite up-link situated in a Member State, or provider uses satellite capacity appertaining to a Member State.

Directive 2014/61 / EU of the European Parliament and of the Council of 15 May 2014 on measures to reduce the cost of installing high-speed electronic communications networks (OJ L 155, 23.5.2014, p. D.2. EU Recommendations and Guidelines:

- *Directive (EU) 2016/1148* of the European Parliament and of the Council of 6 July 2016 on measures for a high level of overall network security and information systems in the EU;

- *Directive 2014/61* / EU of the European Parliament and of the Council of 15 May 2014 on measures to reduce the cost of installing high-speed electronic communications networks ;
- *Decree implementing the Regulation* (EU) on roaming on public mobile communications networks in the EU (Official Gazette of the Republic of Slovenia, No. 55/13 and 28/16);
- *Regulation (EU) 2015/*2120 of the European Parliament and of the Council of 25.11.2015 establishing measures for access to open internet and amending Directive 2002/22 / EC on universal service and users' rights relating to electronic communications networks and services and Regulation (EU) No. 531/2012 on roaming on public mobile communications networks in the EU (OJ L No. 310 of 26.11.2015);
- *Decree implementing the Regulation* (EU) on the definition of measures concerning access to open internet (Official Gazette of the Republic of Slovenia, *No. 29/16)*;
- *Decree implementing the Regulation* (EU) on roaming on public mobile communications networks in the EU (Official Gazette of the Republic of Slovenia, *No. 55/13 and 28/16)*;
- *Regulation (EU) 2015/2120* of the European Parliament and of the Council of 25.11.2015 establishing measures for access to open internet and amending Directive 2002/22 / EC on universal service and users' rights relating to electronic communications networks and services and Regulation (EU) No. 531/2012 on roaming on public mobile communications networks in the EU (OJ L No. 310 of 26.11.2015);
- *Decree implementing the Regulation* (EU) on the definition of measures concerning access to open internet (Official Gazette of the Republic of Slovenia, *No. 29/16)*;

214. Commission recommendation of 20 September 2010 on regulated access to Next Generation Access Networks (NGA) (2010/572/EU)

215. Commission recommendation of 17 December 2007 on relevant product and service markets within the electronic communications sector susceptible to ex ante regulation in accordance with Directive 2002/21/EC of the European Parliament and of the Council on a common regulatory framework for electronic communications networks and services (2007/879/EC)

216. Commission recommendation of 19 September 2005 on accounting separation and cost accounting systems under the regulatory framework for electronic communications (2005/698/EC)

217. Commission guidelines on market analysis and the assessment of significant market power under the Community regulatory framework for electronic communications networks and services (2002/C 165/03)

There are more recommendation and communications in this field:

- European Commission Recommendation of 9 October 2014 on the relevant markets for products and services in the electronic communications sector that may be subject to ex ante regulation in accordance with Directive 2002/21 / EC of the European Parliament and of the Council on a common regulatory framework for electronic communications networks and services (2014/710 / EU);
- European Commission Recommendation of 11 September 2013 on consistent non-discrimination obligations and methodologies for calculating costs to promote competition and improve the environment for broadband investments (2013/466 / EU);
- Communication from the European Commission on the EU guidelines on the application of the state aid rules regarding the rapid deployment of broadband networks;
- Guidelines of the Body of European Regulators for Electronic Communications (BEREC) in the implementation of new rules of neutrality of the internet (2016).

E. Implementation Acts

218. Following, important (not all) implementation acts are listed.

219. Rules on the method of keeping and procedure of entering and on supplying data form media register Official Gazette No. 58/2001, 54/2002 Skl.US: U-I-177/02-5, 94/2002, 73/2003 Odl.US: U-I-177/02-15,

220. Rules on the manner of registration and de-registration of radio and television sets and the manner of paying the user fee for radio and TV programme broadcasting, Official Gazette No. 75/2004 of 13. 7. 2004,

221. Rules on the programmes of special importance Official Gazette No. 85/2002S; These rules lay down precise criteria for the definition of local and regional content, conditions and procedure for obtaining the status of a local or regional, student and non-profit radio and television program;

222. Rules on the criteria for determination of the contents of own production Official Gazette No. 77/02; these rules set out detailed criteria for the definition of programming, produced in accordance with programme requirements by the issuers of radio and television programmes.

223. Decree on the procedure and detailed criteria for acquiring a status of freelance journalist and for keeping the register as public book Ur.l. RS, št. 105/2001

224. Decree on carrying out regular annual tenders for co-financing the creation of programme contents and the development of technical infrastructure in the field of media Official Gazette No. 52/2002, 52/2003

225. Decree on carrying out regular annual tenders for co-financing projects from the budgetary fund for audio-visual media Official Gazette No. 52/2003, 35/2004, 34/2006, 77/2010-ZSFCJA, 1/2011

Some more rules have been enacted:

- *Rules on the Promotion of Investments in Audio-visual Production* (Official Gazette of the Republic of Slovenia, No. 7/17);
- *Rules on the determination of acoustic and visual warnings and a visual symbol for programme contents that are not suitable for children and minors* (Official Gazette of the Republic of Slovenia, No. 50/14);
- *Rules on the implementation of the procedure for the selection of projects, conditions and criteria for the selection of audio-visual projects* (Official Gazette RS, No. 54/12, 43/14 and 43/17).

A number of rules and regulations refer to *AKOS.*[80]

F. Ethical Codes

1. Principles on the Conduct of Journalists

226. IFJ Declaration of Principles on the Conduct of Journalists[81] (This international Declaration is proclaimed as a standard of professional conduct for journalists engaged in gathering, transmitting, disseminating and commenting on news and information in describing events).

227. International Principles of Professional Ethics in Journalism[82] (prepared by international and regional organizations of professional journalists, representing altogether 400,000 working journalists in all parts of the world, as an international common ground and as a source of inspiration for national and regional codes of ethics.

2. Code of Ethics of Slovene Journalists

228. In preparing the new Code of Ethics of Slovene Journalists[83,84] special attention was focused on the IFJ Declaration of Principles on the Conduct of Journalists and the Code of Ethics of the Society of Professional Journalists (SPJ). The first principle of professional conduct of journalists is the right of the public to be informed. Public enlightenment is the basis for the proper functioning of modern

---

80. https://www.akos-rs.si/podzakonski-akti.
81. http://ethicnet.uta.fi/international/declaration_of_principles_on_the_conduct_of_journalists.
82. International+Principles+of+Professional+Ethics+in+Journalism&sourceid=chrome&espv=210&es_sm=93&ie=UTF-8.
83. http://ethicnet.uta.fi/slovenia/code_of_ethics_of_slovene_journalists.
84. https://novinar.com/drustvo/o-nas/dokumenti/kodeks/.

societies and the foundation of democracy. In pursuance of the right of the public to be informed, journalists should at all times, defend the principles of free assembly, disseminating and transmitting information, as well as the right to express opinions.

229. According to Principles on the Conduct of Journalists Principles on the Conduct of Journalists, journalists are obliged to present a comprehensive account of events and – taking into consideration the rights of others – report in an accurate and conscientious manner. Such conduct of journalists is the cornerstone of their credibility. This Code of ethics applies to text, photography, video and audio.

G. Other Related International Acts

230. Act Ratifying the European Trans frontier Television Convention and the Protocol amending the European Trans frontier Television Convention (Official Gazette RS, No. 57/1999), Mednarodne pogodbe (Official Gazette RS, No. 18/1999)

231. Regional agreement relating to the Use of the Band 87.5-108 MHz for FM Sound Broadcasting (Region 1 and Part of Region 3) -English, (Official Gazette RS, No. 5/1997)

232. Regional Radio communication Conference for the revision of the Stockholm 1961 Agreement (RRC-06-Rev.ST61) – English (Official Gazette RS, No. 65/1993)

233. Act Ratifying the Chester 1997 Multilateral Coordination Agreement relating to Technical Criteria, Coordination Principles and Procedures for the introduction of Terrestrial Digital Video Broadcasting (DVB-T) (Official Gazette RS, No. 71/2005), International treaty English (Official Gazette RS, No. 12/2005)

II. Case Law of the Constitutional Court of Slovenia

A. Some Decision of the Constitutional Court Repealed (Official Gazette of the RS, No. 113, 4932/2003)

234. The decision that the implementation of the second and third paragraphs of Article 12 on the MMA and the second paragraph of Article 4 of the Rules on the method of keeping and procedure of entering and on supplying data form media register be suspended until the final decision of the Constitutional Court, No. U-I-177/02-5 of 30 May 2002 (Official Gazette of the Republic of Slovenia No. 54-2655/2002), published on 21 June 2002 and in force since 22 June 2002 stipulates:

235. The implementation of the second and third paragraphs of Article 12 on the MMA (Official Gazette of the Republic of Slovenia No. 35/01) and the second paragraph of Article 4 of the Rules on the method of keeping and procedure of entering and on supplying data form media register (Official Gazette of the Republic of Slovenia No. 58/01) be suspended until the final decision of the Constitutional Court.

236. With this decision of the Constitutional Court, its Decision of 30 May 2002 on the suspension of the implementation of the second sentence of the third paragraph of ZMed and the second paragraph of Article 4 of the Rules shall cease to be valid.

The Decision of the Constitutional Court No. U-I-177/02-15 of 10 July 2003 (Official Gazette of the Republic of Slovenia No. 73-3559/2003)

237. The Decision of the Constitutional Court No. U-I-177/02-15 of 10 July 2003, that the second sentence of the third paragraph of Article 12 and the first paragraph of Article 150 of the MMA and the second paragraph of Article 4 of the Rules on the method of keeping and procedure of entering and on supplying data form media register are not incompliant with the Constitution (Official Gazette of the Republic of Slovenia No. 73-3559/2003), published on 29 July 2003 and valid since 30 July 2003 also stipulates:

238. The second and third paragraphs of Article 12 and the first paragraph of Article 150 of the MMA (Official Gazette of the Republic of Slovenia No. 35/01) and the second paragraph of Article 4 of the Rules on the method of keeping and procedure of entering and on supplying data form media register (Official Gazette of the Republic of Slovenia No. 58/01) are not incompliant with the Constitution.

The Decision of the Constitutional Court No. U-I-188/01-12 of 16 November 2003 on the repeal of Article 107 of the MMA (Official Gazette of the Republic of Slovenia No. 113-4932/2003)

239. The Decision of the Constitutional Court No. U-I-188/01-12 of 16 November 2003 on the repeal of Article 107 of the MMA (Official Gazette of the Republic of Slovenia No. 113-4932/2003), published on 20 November 2003 and valid since 21 November 2003 stipulates:

> 'Article 107 of the MMA (Official Gazette of the Republic of Slovenia, nos. 35/01 and 62/03) is hereby repealed.'

The Decision of the Constitutional Court No. U-I-106/01-27 of 5 February 2004 (Official Gazette of the Republic of Slovenia No. 16-648/2004)

240. The Decision of the Constitutional Court No. U-I-106/01-27 of 5 February 2004 on partial repeal of Article 82 of the MMA and on repeal of the Rules on the criteria for the financing of programme of radio and television programme services with the status of a local, regional or student radio or television programme service

(Official Gazette of the Republic of Slovenia No. 16-648/2004), published on 20 February 2004, valid since 21 February 2004 and in effect since 20 September 2004 also stipulates:

241. The words 'and the RTV licence fee' in the first paragraph of Article 82 and the second paragraph of Article 82 of the MMA (Official Gazette of the Republic of Slovenia No. 35/01) shall be repealed.

242. The repeal from points 1 and 3 of the operative part shall take effect seven months after the publication of this Decision in the Official Gazette of the Republic of Slovenia.

The Decision of the Constitutional Court No. U-I-207/01-20 of 28 October 2004 (Official Gazette of the Republic of Slovenia No. 123-5132/2004)

243. The Decision of the Constitutional Court No. U-I-207/01-20 of 28 October 2004 on the repeal of the sixth and the seventh paragraph of Article 112 of the MMA (Official Gazette of the Republic of Slovenia No. 123-5132/2004), published on 18 November 2004 and valid since 19 November 2004 also stipulates:

> The sixth and the seventh paragraph of Article 112 of the MMA (Official Gazette of the Republic of Slovenia, No. 35/01) are hereby repealed.

The authentic explanation of the first and the third paragraph of Article 84 of the MMA – ORZMed84 (Official Gazette of the Republic of Slovenia No. 62-3026/2003)

244. The authentic explanation of the first and the third paragraph of Article 84 of the MMA – ORZMed84 (Official Gazette of the Republic of Slovenia No. 62-3026/2003), published on 27 June 2003 and in force since 27 June 2003 is the following:

> Pursuant to the first paragraph of Article 84 of the Mass Media Act, it is prohibited to broadcast the programmes that could seriously harm the mental, moral or physical development of children and other minors, namely, it is prohibited to broadcast the scenes of unjust violence such as torturing of people, animals and similar, pornography, such as zoophilia, necrophilia, paedophilia, sadomasochism, sadism, rape and other abominations and scenes of violence in pornography or other programmes that could severely harm the mental, moral or physical development of children and minors.

245. The text of the third paragraph hereunder shall be interpreted in such a way that the programmes hereunder are programmes that could severely harm the mental, moral or physical development of children and minors which is why it shall be prohibited to broadcast them outside the time period between midnight and 5 a.m.

so that it would mostly be impossible for the children and minors to see them. These programmes include all those that contain the scenes of sexuality or violence which can be classified as falling within the socially acceptable aesthetic and moral criteria and which are not prohibited in accordance with the first paragraph hereunder.

The Decision of the Constitutional Court, finding that the third paragraph of Article 169 and the fourth paragraph of Article 171 of the Criminal Code are not inconsistent with the Constitution (Official Gazette of RS, No. 60/1999, 7 of 29, 1999)

246. The petitioner challenged provisions of the third paragraph of Article 169, fourth and sixth paragraphs of Article 171 and the fifth paragraph of Article 172 of the PC. The impugned provisions were supposed to be contrary to the principle of equality before the law (Article 14 of the Constitution). The court decided, that petitioners' allegation that the challenged provisions contrary to the principle of equality before the law (Article 14 of the Constitution) exclude the criminalization of certain interventions in the individual's honour and good name, is not well founded. According to the court it is also not justified petitioners' allegation that the challenged provisions of the Criminal Code in conflict with the third paragraph of Article 15 of the Constitution regulate the conflict between the right to personal dignity (Article 34 of the Constitution) and the guarantee of the inviolability of personal rights (Article 35 of the Constitution) on the one hand and freedom of expression (Article 39) on the other.

Part I. Freedom of Speech

§1. Constitutional Framework

I. General on Media Related Rights and Freedoms

· *247.* *Freedom of speech* is the political right with its origin that dates back much before contemporary concepts of human rights (ancient Athens in the late 6th or early 5th century).

248. The modern history of freedom of speech is as long as the history of democratic societies.[85] Historical documents of human civilization like the *Bill of Rights*, the *Magna Charta*, the *Petition of Right*, the *Habeas Corpus Act*, *Convention for the Protection of Human Rights* and Fundamental Freedoms and many others including contemporary ones as for ex. *The European Convention on Human Rights* never avoided this issue. Or, for example, European.

249. Convention on Trans frontier Television that considers the freedom of expression and information constitutes one of the essential principles of a democratic society and one of the basic conditions for its progress and for the development of every human being.

250. Modern constitutions are following the famous provision *of* Article 10 of the European Convention on Human Rights (hereinafter the Convention).[86] The Convention provides that everyone has the *right to freedom of expression*. This right includes freedom to hold opinions and to receive and impart information and ideas without interference by public authority and regardless of frontiers.

251. But, as it is explicitly stipulated in the Convention, this *right is not without limitations* and restrictions. The exercise of these freedoms, since it carries with it duties and responsibilities, may be subject to such formalities, conditions, restrictions or penalties as are prescribed by law and are necessary in a democratic society, in the interests of national security, territorial integrity or public safety, for the

85. The Bill of Rights is an Act of the Parliament of England passed on 16 Dec. 1689 stipulated, that the freedom of speech and debates or proceedings in Parliament ought not to be impeached or questioned in any court or place out of Parliament. In the United Kingdom, the Bill of Rights is further accompanied by the Magna Carta, the Petition of Right, the Habeas Corpus Act 1679.

86. Article 10 of The European Convention on Human Rights and Fundamental Freedoms, Rome 4 Nov. 1950 and its Five Protocols.

prevention of disorder or crime, for the protection of health or morals, for the protection of the reputation or the rights of others, for preventing the disclosure of information received in confidence, or for maintaining the authority and impartiality of the judiciary. It is explicitly stipulated, that the provision on the right to freedom of expression, does not prevent States from requiring the licensing of broadcasting, television or cinema enterprises.

252. Constitutional and legal regulation on freedom of speech in Slovenia is fully in line with Article 17 of the United Nations International Covenant on Civil and Political Rights[87] which states:

> 1. No one shall be subjected to arbitrary or unlawful interference with his privacy, family, home or correspondence, nor to unlawful attacks on his honour and reputation.
>
> 2. Everyone has the right to the protection of the law against such interference or attacks.

253. It is also in line with Article 10 of the European Convention on Human Rights (ECHR)[88] that permits restrictions on freedom of speech when necessary to protect the reputation or rights of others. Namely, Article 10 of ECHR stipulates, that everyone has the right to freedom of expression (includes freedom to hold opinions and to receive and impart information and ideas without interference by public authority and regardless of frontiers). But, as the Convention explicitly stipulates, this provision does not mean, that States are prevented from requiring the licensing of broadcasting, television or cinema enterprises.

254. ECHR also explicitly provides that the exercise of these freedoms, since it carries with it duties and responsibilities, may be subject to such *formalities, conditions, restrictions or penalties* as are prescribed by law and are necessary in a democratic society. Limitations are in the interests of national security, territorial integrity or public safety, for the prevention of disorder or crime, for the protection of health or morals, for the protection of the reputation or the rights of others, for preventing the disclosure of information received in confidence, or for maintaining the authority and impartiality of the judiciary (Article 10 of the ECHR).

255. There is no uniform answer in legislations to find the equilibrium between the two values. Jurisdictions resolve this tension in different ways, in particular in determining where the burden of proof lies when unfounded allegations are made. The power of the internet to disseminate comment, which may include malicious comment, has brought a new focus to the issue.[89]

---

87. United Nations International Covenant on Civil and Political Rights: http://www.hrweb.org/legal/cpr.html.
88. European Convention on Human Rights: http://www.echr.coe.int/Documents/Convention_ENG.pdf.
89. Read more: http://www.pressreference.com/knowledge/Defamation.html#ixzz2xzQmLShq.

256. Slovenia' legislation mainly follows the observations and recommendations of the human rights organizations, and other organizations such as the Council of Europe and Organization for Security and Cooperation in Europe with respect to implementation of the freedom of expression. Slovenia also follows the jurisprudence of The European Court of Human Rights (that refers to the freedom of expression provisions of the European Convention on Human Rights) and adjusts its legislation respectively (e.g., *Lingens v. Austria* (1986).

II. Media Related Rights and Freedoms in the Constitution of Slovenia

257. Slovenian Constitution is completely in accordance with the above provision *of* The European Convention on Human Rights. *Freedom of expression* and the *Right to correction and reply* are Constitutional freedom and right according to Constitution of Slovenia. Article 39 of the Constitution of Slovenia stipulates freedom of expression as one of the fundamental Constitutional freedoms. Freedom of expression encompasses *freedom of thought, freedom of speech and freedom of public appearance.* Freedom of expression further on includes *freedom of the press and other forms of public communication and expression.* According to the Constitution of Slovenia freedom of expression shall be guaranteed.

258. Constitution of Slovenia guarantees everyone to *freely collect, receive and disseminate information and opinions.* Except in such cases as are provided by law, everyone has the right to obtain information of a public nature in which he/she has a well-founded legal interest under law (Article 39 of the Constitution of Slovenia).

259. The *right to correct published information* which has damaged a right or interest of an individual, organization or body is guaranteed, as it is the *right to reply to such published information* (Article 40 of the Constitution of Slovenia).Both rights (Correction and Reply) are in details elaborated in the respective Law on Mass Media.

§2. Scope

I. Freedom of Expression in the MMA

260. According to the law, mass media activities in Slovenia are based on protection of the Slovene language, *freedom of expression*, freedom of dissemination of programme from other countries and prohibition of incitement to inequality and intolerance.

261. Mass media activities in Slovenia are based on freedom of expression, the inviolability and protection of *human personality and dignity*, the free flow of information, media *openness* to different opinions and beliefs and to diverse content, the *autonomy* of editorial personnel, journalists and other authors/creators in creating programme in accordance with programme concepts and professional codes of behaviour, and the *personal responsibility* of journalists, other authors/creators of pieces and editorial personnel for the consequences of their work (Article 6 of the MMA).

262. The Republic of Slovenia in its territory ensure *freedom in disseminating* and receiving programme from other countries, and may in individual cases restrict such freedom only in accordance with an international treaty by which the Republic of Slovenia is bound, and with the MMA (Article 7 of the MMA).

263. The dissemination of programme that encourages national, racial, religious, sexual or any other *inequality, or violence and war, or incites* national, racial, religious, sexual or any other hatred and intolerance is prohibited (MMA, Article 8).

II. The Right to Public Information and to Be Informed

264. The right to public information and to be informed is further elaborated in the law. Article 4 of the MMA, sets out *the right of citizens to public information* and *to be informed in general.* The same right belongs equally to Slovenes around the world, members of the Slovene minorities in Austria, Hungary and Italy, the Hungarian and Italian ethnic communities in Slovenia, and the Romani community living in Slovenia.

265. The Republic of Slovenia supports the *plurality and diversification* of the mass media, the protection of the Slovenian national and cultural identity, the promotion of cultural creativity in the area of the mass media and a culture of public dialogue. The Republic of Slovenia supports the mass media for the consolidation of the *social state* based on the *rule of law* and the development of education and science (Article 4 of the MMA).

III. Right to Correction in MMA

266. Section 6 of the MMA regulates Constitutional right to correction *of a report published.* The term *report is to be understood broadly; it means any kind of publication* by which the rights or interests of an individual, organization or body may be infringed upon, regardless of whether such contents have been published as a news flash, comment or any other form.

267. The term *correction is to be understood broadly* as well; it entails *not only* a correction *in the narrow sense*, i.e. the negation or correction of erroneous or untrue statements in the published report, but also any *citation or presentation of other or contradictory facts and circumstances* by which the person infringed upon disproves the statements in the report published, or significantly adds thereto for the purpose of disproval.

268. Article 26 of the MMA declares that any person has the right to demand that the responsible editor publish free of charge a correction by such person to any report published that infringed upon the person's rights or interests. The publication of the correction may be requested *within 30 days from the day the person concerned learned* of the publication of the notice, but no later than three months after the publication of the notice (amended Article 26 of the MMA, 2016).

IV. The Way of Publishing the Correction

269. According to Article 27 of the MMA, the correction must be published *without substantive amendments or supplements.* Only spelling corrections are allowed, provided that the person affected had been informed of and *agreed* to them. Each such publication must be *clearly marked as 'correction'* or, alternatively, the indication '*presentation of contradictory facts*'. The publication must contain the name of the affected person and the reference to the relevant article or programme.

270. The correction must be published in such *form and place* that its publication has the same value as the article or the contribution to which it refers. If there are several issues or programmes of a media, the correction must be published in those issues or programmes in which the article or the contribution has been published which the correction or the presentation of contradictory facts refers to. If a correction refers to two or more notices covering the same event or the same person and having been published in different media of the same publisher/broadcaster, the correction must be published in all those media.

V. The Time of Publishing the Correction

271. Correction must be published if the medium is *issued once a month* or in even longer time intervals and the request for the publishing is received at least 14 days before the issue *in the first next issue* or programme after receiving the correction. In all other cases correction must be published *no later than in the second issue* or the corresponding programme of the medium after receiving the correction. In *electronic publications* correction must be published *within 48 hours* after receiving the correction (Article 27 of the MMA).

VI. Correction in Printed Media

272. In printed media it is deemed that a correction has been published on an appropriate site if published *on the same page of the same column*, using the same font type and size as the article it refers to. If the original article has been published on the front page of a newspaper, a *warning on the front page* saying that the correction is published inside the printed medium is sufficient. The warning on the front page must clearly state that this is a correction and must contain at least the subject of negation or presentation of contradictory facts and, in case the name of the affected person has been published in the original article, also such name. If the claim the correction refers to had been stated in the title, it is deemed that the correction had been published on the same or equivalent site if the title of the correction is placed in the same area as the title of the article it refers to. In case a warning is published on the front page, such warning must cover at least an area of the same size as that covered by the title of the article such correction refers to (Article 27 of the MMA).

VII. Correction in Radio or Television Programme

273. Publication in *a radio or television programme* service and other technically equivalent programmes *must be read*. If the original text in these programmes was repeated, a single publication of the correction in the prime time is sufficient. If the original contribution was accompanied by a picture, the correction must also be accompanied by such picture. The responsible editor of the medium must inform the affected person in which issue or programme the requested correction would be published, or alternatively, that such publication is rejected, within 24 hours of receiving the correction. If the responsible editor rejects the publication of the correction, such decision must be justified in writing. The explanation must clearly and unambiguously say which statements in the corrections gave rise to such rejection (Article 27 of the MMA).

274. Any person who demands the publication of a correction or presentation of contradictory facts must, according to Article 28 of the MMA, cite the report to which the correction relates and the date it was published. The title of the correction must also be given. In case no title is given of a correction or such title is not evident from the wording of the correction, it must be determined by the responsible editor. A commentary on or response to a correction may not be published simultaneously in the same issue or programme of the mass medium.

VIII. Keeping the Record

275. Article 29 of the MMA stipulates, that the responsible editor must keep written records of all programme published for at least fifteen days after its publication, and deliver an appropriate copy of the particular record to a person with a legitimate interest at that person's expense within three days of receiving written request therefrom. Copies may be delivered to persons with a legitimate interest for exclusively personal use. They may not be reproduced or published without the consent of the publisher/broadcaster, except within the framework of court proceedings.

276. If within eight days of the publication of a report the person concerned makes a written declaration that the publication of a correction is to be demanded, the responsible editor must in accordance with the Article 32 of the MMA, keep a written record of the report for which the correction is demanded until court proceedings are completed.

IX. Legal Ground for Rejection

277. The responsible editor must, according to Article 31 of the MMA publish a correction, except in the following cases:

- if the correction demanded does not relate to the report to which the person concerned refers;
- if the required correction in no respect denies the statements in the report, and does not give or present any other or contradictory facts or circumstances by means of which the affected person would disprove or significantly add thereto for the purpose of disproval;
- if the publication of the correction would be in contravention of law;
- if a demand from a state body or legal entity for the publication of a correction is not signed by the responsible officer or a person authorized for the contacts with the public by such state body or legal entity;
- if the correction is worded in an offensive manner;
- if the correction demanded is disproportionately longer that the report in which the statements for which is being given were made, or than the section of the report to which it directly relates;
- if the demand for the publication of a correction was lodged after the expiry of the period specified by MMA;
- if the content of the correction demanded is the same as that of a correction demanded about which a case before a court is proceeding owing to the rejection or unsuitability of the form of publication.

278. The responsible editor must decide on the rejection of such correction within 24 hours and send the decision on rejection to the person who demanded the publication of the correction via registered mail.

X. The Right to File a Suit Against the Responsible Editor

279. If the responsible editor fails to publish a correction within the defined period and in the manner stipulated by MMA the person that demanded the publication of the correction has according to the Article 33 of the MMA *the* right to *file a suit against the responsible editor*. The court *competent court is* the court for civil disputes in the area of the head office or permanent residence of the publisher/broadcaster of the mass medium through which the report to which the correction relates was published. A suit may be filed within thirty days of the expiry of the deadline for publishing the correction, or of the day on which the correction was published in a manner not in accordance with the MMA.

XI. The Court Procedure

280. The procedure stipulated by law (Article 34 of the MMA) is *fast*; defendant must respond to the suit within 8 days of its receipt. The first main hearing must be carried out no later than 45 days after the filing of the suit with the court. The proceeding before the court has priority. The ruling must be served to the parties involved within three months of filing the suit.

281. Trials involving a suit for the publication of a correction are *limited to hearing and demonstrating the facts* on which the defendants obligation to publish a correction depends. In disputes concerning the publication of a correction the court rejects the claim if it is determined that the rights or interests of the plaintiff have not been infringed upon, or if any other circumstances have been given owing to which under law the correction need not be published.

282. The institution of criminal proceedings because of an act committed through the publication of the report to which the correction relates, according to Article 36 of the MMA, does not suspend the procedure for publication of the correction. If, after a suit is filed at the court, the responsible *editor of the mass medium is replaced*, the plaintiff may, according to Article 37 of the MMA, amend the suit before the end of the trial and sue the new responsible editor in place of the original defendant. It is not necessary to obtain the consent of the original defendant or the new responsible editor for such an amendment to the suit.

283. The court must, pursuant to Article 38, pronounce *judgment within three days* of the end of the trial. The court has to deliver an authentic copy of the judgment to the parties within three days of pronouncing judgment. If the court finds for the plaintiff, it orders the defendant in *the judgment to publish a correction* within the period and in the manner stipulated by law. In publishing the correction the responsible editor must state that it is a matter of publication on the basis of a judgment and cite the judgment proper.

284. The parties may, following the Article 39 of the MMA file an *appeal at a higher court* against a judgment from the court of first instance within three days of its delivery. An appeal is delivered to the opposing party for response. A legitimate appeal submitted on time is sent by the court of first instance with all accompanying dossiers to the court of second instance within two days of being filed. The court of second instance must rule on an appeal within three days of receiving the appeal and dossiers. A legal review is permitted against a judgment by the court of second instance.

XII. Right to Reply to Information Published

285. According to Article 42 of the MMA, the right to reply is intended *to secure the interest of the public* in terms of objective, multilateral and up-to-date information, as one of the essential conditions for democratic decision-making in public affairs; it is stipulated by the MMA, that any person has the right to demand that the responsible editor *publish free of charge a reply to information* published by which that person through demonstrable statements denies, significantly corrects or significantly elaborates upon the statement of facts and figures in the information published.

286. Replies must be, according to Article 43 of the MMA, published *without substantive amendments* or additions, with the exception of grammatical corrections. The responsible editor has the right to request prior to publication an abridgement of the reply by the author. The provisions on the legal grounds for rejection of the publication of correction (Article 31) of the MMA applies to a reply, whereby the responsible editor may reject the publication of replies of the same content when a single reply has already been published. The responsible editor may also reject the publication of a reply if the reply cites untrue or indemonstrable information or assertions. If in the opinion of the responsible editor only certain information or assertions are untrue or indemonstrable, the responsible editor may not reject publication without first calling upon the author to withdraw such information or assertions from the reply.

XIII. Criticism on Media Freedom in Slovenia

287. Despite the above described endeavours, the international assessment of *Media Independence* in Slovenia is still not satisfactory. According to *FREEDOM HOUSE Report 2012*, journalists in Slovenia continue to experience political pressure and harassment in the form of defamation suits by public figures. Slovenia's rating for independent media remains at 2.50.[90]

288. In autumn 2007, 571 journalists signed the *Petition against censorship and political pressures on journalists in Slovenia* as an expression of protest against interference of politics in the media, saying, and media freedom in Slovenia remains restricted. By the Petition, as 571 journalists signatories have issued, as they declare, a warning against censorship and political pressures, but its government and the Parliament still reject any dialogue with the journalists.

289. Two of the initiators of the Petition Blaž Zgaga and Matej Šurc on 31 December 2007 wrote an *Open letter at the beginning of Slovenian presidency* of the EU, criticizing among others that the Radio and Television Act, passed in 2005, has essentially degraded public radio and television. According to them, the leading positions have been occupied by pro-government oriented but mostly incompetent people and consequently many well-known journalists have left these institutions, and violations of basic premises of journalist profession are on the increase.[91]

---

90. http://www.freedomhouse.org/report/nations-transit/2012/slovenia#.Uz-9cU2KD3g.
91. The contents of the cited letter: http://www.humanrightspoint.si/files/att/media/Open%20letter%20Zgaga%20Surc.pdf.

290. According to Human Rights Media Watch, from 2009, t*he problems concerning media freedom and journalists' autonomy* in Slovenia have escalated between 2005 and 2007 around the controversial media regulation changes and takeovers of several daily newspapers, the public service radio and television and the press agency. In those media the governing bodies, managers, editors and reporters, mostly those reporting politics, home affairs, foreign affairs and security have been in many cases replaced by the professionals reliable to the political parties in power. In the period of politically motivated takeovers of the media many journalists have been exposed to censorship, pressure, degradation, to formal and informal sanctions. In number of cases, especially in those taking place in the biggest daily Delo, professional associations of journalists have been engaged in legal defence of professional autonomy and labour rights of journalists.[92]

291. 2006 changes of *media regulation* have introduced stricter rules on right of reply which contribute to restriction of editorial freedom. 2005 changes of regulation of public service broadcasting caused major conflicts and have been approved at referendum with very tight vote in favour of the regulation. Introduction of increased involvement of the Parliament and the government in appointments of the governing bodies of public service radio and television has been criticized by several European organizations, including the Council of Europe.[93]

292. Beside problems arising from relations between politics and the media, also *conflicts between journalists and publishers* have had negative impact on media freedom and autonomy of journalists in Slovenia. Disagreements concerning collective agreement for journalists and employment policy of publishers (which is increasingly preferring temporary contracts and fake freelance arrangements) caused even journalists' strike on the elections day in October 2004. The disagreements despite negotiations haven't been solved yet.

293. With regard to legal conditions for the work of journalists it is important to mention that *defamation is defined as both civil and criminal offence*. The PC determines sanctions for such criminal offence even in the form of penalty of imprisonment for up to one year. In principle, the liability lies with the author or journalist, unless he or she is unknown, in which case the liability lies with the editor or the particular media entity. The upper limit of civil compensation is not defined by law. There have been proposals to limit or abolish the criminal liability of journalists in Slovenia; however recent initiatives to amend the PC don't include such solution.[94]

294. Under the provision of the media law editors, journalists and other authors who publish in the media are protected from disclosure of sources. However, it is

92. Human Rights Press Point: http://www.humanrightspoint.si/node/7.
93. *Ibid.*
94. *Ibid.*

not possible to appeal for the protection of the source of information in penal proceedings. The Supreme Court sentenced the state to pay compensation to a journalist whose list of phone calls was reviewed by the police several years ago without the court order, after he refused to disclose his source.

§3. No A Priori Censorship

295. No a priori Censorship is introduced in Slovenian media legal system. Mass media activities in Slovenia are based on *freedom of expression*, the inviolability and protection of human personality and dignity, the free flow of information, media openness to different opinions and beliefs and to diverse content, the autonomy of editorial personnel, journalists and other authors/creators in creating programme in accordance with programme concepts and professional codes of behaviour, and the personal responsibility of journalists, other *authors/creators* of pieces and editorial personnel for the consequences of their work (Article 6 of the MMA).

296. The Republic of Slovenia in its territory ensure freedom in disseminating and receiving programme from other countries, and may in individual cases restrict such freedom only in accordance with an international treaty by which the Republic of Slovenia is bound, and with the MMA (Article 7).

297. But there is a number of rules and principles, that must be respected in order to respect Constitutional freedoms of expression and right to be informed. For ex. the dissemination of programme that encourages national, racial, religious, sexual or any other inequality, or violence and war, or incites national, racial, religious, sexual or any other hatred and intolerance is prohibited (MMA, Article 8).

298. According to the law, mass media activities in Slovenia are based on protection of the *Slovene language, freedom of expression, freedom of dissemination* of programme from other countries and prohibition of incitement to inequality and intolerance. The dissemination of programme that encourages national, racial, religious, sexual or any other inequality, or violence and war, or incites national, racial, religious, sexual or any other hatred and intolerance shall be prohibited (MMA, Article 8).

§4. Spectrum of a Posteriori Restrictive Measures

299. There are a number of so-called a posteriori restrictive measures. Let us take as example general principles defined by AVMSA[95] like:

95. Official Gazette No. 87/2011 of 19 Oct. 2011, AVMS, Slov.: Zakon o avdiovizualnih medijskih storitvah, ZAMS.

- *Prohibition of Incitement to Discrimination and Intolerance* (Article 9); It is prohibited to promote national, racial, religious, sexual or other discrimination, violence and war, or incite national, racial, religious, sexual or other hatred and intolerance by means of audio-visual media services. It is also prohibited to undermine the respect for human dignity by means of audio-visual media services.
- *Protection of Children and Adolescents* (Article 10); Children and adolescents enjoy special protection under Audio-Visual Media Services (AVMS). The interests of children *and* adolescents have priority over all other rights and considerations. It is prohibited to undermine the physical, mental or moral development of children and adolescents by means of AVMS. Children or adolescents must not be exposed to arbitrary or unlawful interference with their private life, family or home, or to unlawful attacks on their honour and reputation by means of AVMS.
- *Protection of vulnerable social groups* (Article 11)*;* In accordance with the law governing the media, the Republic of Slovenia encourages providers to progressively provide access to their services for visually and hearing impaired persons. In accordance with the law governing the media, the Republic of Slovenia promotes media literacy in terms of skill, knowledge and understanding that enable an efficient and safe use of media and AVMS.
- *Freedom of dissemination of AVMS from other* countries (Article 12); The Republic of Slovenia ensures freedom of reception and dissemination of AVMS from other EU Member States and does not restrict their transmissions on its territory, except in cases specified in Articles 3 and 4 of Directive 2010/13/EU.
- *Right to correction and reply* (Article 13); the AVMS guarantee the right to correction and reply in accordance with the law governing the media.

300. Violations of the above principles are penalized by criminal sanctions and damage liability under respective legislation.

§5. No Prior Authorization for Publishing

301. There is of course no prior authorization for publishing, but there are number of legal institutes to prevent violation of rights and freedoms and right to be informed and other rights and freedoms in the field of media. For example, Article 42 of the MMA, the right to reply, is intended *to secure the interest of the public* in terms of objective, multilateral and up-to-date information, as one of the essential conditions for democratic decision-making in public affairs.

Part II. Regulation of Print Media

Chapter 1. The Journalists' Profession

§1. Notion

I. Journalist

302. It is not much said on journalists in the MMA. It is only defined, that under the law (MMA, Article 21) a journalist is any person who is involved in the collection, processing, structuring or sorting of *information for publication via the mass media* and is *employed at a publisher/broadcaster*; in addition a journalist is also a person, who performs journalistic activities *independently as an occupation* (a freelance journalist).

303. Ethical and professional principles of journalists profession are in more elaborated manner, as a recommendation way set out in the *Code of Ethics of Slovene Journalists*[96] (hereinafter Code). Of course, all rules and principles related to journalists' profession are applicable for both, for journalists in *printed media* as well as the journalists in *broadcasting media*. A special new type of journalists occurred in recent years, namely, *online journalists.*

II. Freelance Journalists

304. The status of freelance journalists (MMA, Article 22) can be acquired through an entry in the *register of freelance journalists* at the relevant ministry, following expression of a prior opinion by a registered professional journalists' organization. Any person who *performs journalistic activities* as a sole or principal occupation and has proof of publication in mass media, who holds a *certificate on active knowledge of Slovene* (for non-citizens) *and has not been banned* from performing such activities by a legally binding court ruling may be entered in the register.

305. Government of the Republic of Slovenia via a *decree prescribes the procedure and detailed criteria* for acquiring the status of a freelance journalist and for administering the register of freelance journalists as a pubic book of record and the

96. http://ethicnet.uta.fi/slovenia/code_of_ethics_of_slovene_journalists.

method and procedure for periodic verification of the fulfilment of the conditions that must be fulfilled by a freelance journalist for entry in the register shall be set out.

306. For most young, highly educated individuals who see their future in journalism profession is increasingly difficult to obtain the first job, and they were forced to work as part-time associates who have no social security. For this reason, it is defined in the National Programme for Culture 2014–2017, that the freelance journalists are those reporters who cannot/do not want to get a regular job, but are forced to/want to work with several different media through various contractual forms that provide the means of subsistence. Freelance journalist is both, those young, highly educated independent journalists who are starting their professional career and their scope of work does not provide sufficient funds for a minimum of social security, while showing promising results, as well as senior independent journalists who demonstrate superior results.[97]

III. Online Journalists

307. As indicated earlier, a new type of journalists occurred in recent years, namely so-called *online journalists.* Their position is still as well weak as the position of digital media in the media market.

308. Inside the Slovenian journalistic community, journalists are polarized into 'defenders' and 'critics' of online journalism, whereas online journalists are often not regarded as 'real' journalists due to their mostly repackaging content. Furthermore, half of about 120 online journalists have fixed-term contracts, more than a third of them are students and slightly more than 10% have regular and open-ended employment. This means that that a large majority of Slovenian online journalists are what International Federation of Journalists (IFJ) regard as 'atypical media workers'.[98]

IV. General Ethical Norms

309. General ethical and professional norms applicable to journalists are defined in the Code. According to Code, the journalist should respect the *individual's right to privacy* and avoid sensationalistic and unjustified disclosure to the public of anyone's privacy. Intrusion into an individual's privacy is only permissible if there is an overriding *public interest.* With public officials and others seeking power, influence and attention, *the public's right to be informed* is greater. The journalist should

97. The National Program for Culture 2014 – 2017, adopted in 2013 by the National Assembly at the proposal of the government.
98. Igor Vobič, Faculty of Social Sciences, University of Ljubljana, Slovenia, Marko Milosavljević Faculty of Social Sciences, University of Ljubljana Slovenia, Media Landscape of Slovenia.

be aware that gathering and publishing information and photographs may cause harm to individuals not accustomed to media and public attention.

310. Code further stipulates that when reporting on judicial matters, the journalist should take into consideration that *no one is guilty until legally found so*. The journalist should exercise caution in publishing names and photographs of perpetrators, victims and their relatives when reporting on tragedies and pre-trial proceedings.

311. Code stipulates, that the journalist should be tactful when gathering and reporting information, publishing photographs and transmitting statements on *children and minors,* those affected by misfortune or family tragedy, the physically or mentally disabled and others having severe handicaps or illnesses. The journalist should, according to the Code, avoid stereotyping by race, gender, age, religion, ethnicity, geography, sexual orientation, disability, physical appearance and social status. *Discrimination* based on sex, ethnicity, religion, social or national origins, insults about religious feelings and customs and incitement of conflicts between nationalities is *not permissible.*

V. Journalistic Work

312. According to Code, the journalist should *verify the accuracy* of information gathered and exercise care to avoid mistakes. Each mistake – however, inadvertently – should be admitted and corrected. When publishing information involving *serious allegations*, the journalist should, according to Code, try to receive a response from those affected. When publishing unconfirmed information or speculation, this should be expressly pointed out by the journalist.

313. Code explicitly stipulates that the journalist should *not conceal essential information* he/she has gathered or falsify documents. Montages, announcements, titles and subtitles should not misrepresent the content. Symbolic and archive material should be labelled accordingly. Code explicitly forbids plagiarism; it is said, that plagiarism is not permissible.

314. Also, according to Code, the journalist should *distinguish between news and commentary.* The distinction between a factual report and commentary should be clearly defined. If involved in the events, Code stipulates, that the journalist reports on, he/she should disclose this or exclude himself/herself as a journalist.

VI. Conflicts of Interest

315. According to Code, interweaving or *combining journalistic and advertising* texts and actions is not permissible. Advertisements, paid announcements and commercials should be clearly and unambiguously distinguished from journalistic texts. If there is any possibility of misunderstanding or doubt, an advertisement should be unambiguously labelled as such. Hybrids that blur the line between advertising and journalistic contents are not permissible.

316. The journalist should, according to Code, avoid situations that might lead to real or perceived conflicts of interest, which might compromise his/her integrity or that of the journalistic community. To avoid real or perceived conflicts of interest, the journalist should, according to Code, *refuse gifts, favours and fees, and shun free travel, special treatment, secondary employment, political involvement, public office and service in community organizations* if this might diminish his/her credibility or that of the journalistic community.

317. The journalist should *not take private advantage of the information* on financial events gained in the course of his/her duties. If the journalist trades in stocks he/she reports on, this should be disclosed to the public. The journalist is, according to Code, obliged to *refuse benefits offered to him/her* by advertisers or special interests and to resist their attempts to influence his/her news coverage. The journalist should *disclose possible unavoidable conflicts* of interest to the public or exclude himself/herself from reporting and commenting on them.

§2. Subsidies to the Press

I. General on Budgetary Funding of the Media

318. The Republic of Slovenia provides for the budgetary funds for the mass media for the implementation of the state aid in exercising the *public interest in the mass media.* The Republic of Slovenia provides the funds also for assuring *plurality and democracy of general informative printed media* (Article 4a of the MMA).

II. Co-financing of the Printed Media

319. When discussing the *co-financing of the general informative printed media*, the basic criteria is that the respective print media are assuring regular, *objective and balanced* presentations of the political activities and positions of various organizations and individuals, especially the political coalition and opposition. In addition, there are the *criteria* of quality, originality, communication and topicality of author's treatment, further on the average number of sold copies of printed media and average number of published original articles in the individual issue.

320. The volume of general informative, cultural, scientific, professional, research and educational programme contents and the significance for the exercising of the right to public information and to be informed objectively is also relevant criteria. Assuring *more jobs* or employments for the journalists or the programme staff who help create the medium and overall significance for a region or a local community is also relevant in decision-making on the financial support of print media.

Chapter 2. Journalists' Rights

§1. Role of Journalists as Watchdogs of Society

321. In addition to rights, duties and social position of journalists stipulated and guaranteed by media legislation (*independence, freedom of expression, autonomy, accountability to the public, penal and damage liability*), there are respective provisions in the Code. Code determines that the journalist is obliged to abide by the same standards to which he/she holds others.

322. Nobody has the right to force a journalist to act contrary to his/her conviction. According to the Code, the journalist has the right *to turn down any job, which is contrary to the Code* or his/her convictions. As it is said in the Code, *no one is allowed to alter or revise the content* of the journalist's report or other pieces of work without his/her consent. The journalist has the right to sign his/her piece of work, and it may not be signed without his/her knowledge or against his/her will.

323. Should the journalist be invited to a session of the Journalists' Ethics Council, he/she is, according to Code, *obliged to attend* it and to abide by its adjudications. In professional matters, the journalist should recognize as competent the judgment of his/her colleagues only.

§2. Journalists' Independence

I. Written Press

324. The scope of journalists' independence is regulated by law generally for *both printed and broadcasting* (including digital) media. According to the MMA, the editorial board, editorial personnel, journalists, and authors/creators of other programme pieces are *independent in their work* within the framework of the programme concept and in accordance with the publisher's/broadcasters basic legal act (MMA, Article 21).

325. Journalists' independence and freedom of expression are also legally protected in their status as employees or as contract partners in performing their duties as journalists. Namely, *journalists may not have their employment terminated,* or a contracted concluded with them cancelled, neither their pay reduced, nor their status in the editorial board changed or their position worsened in any other manner for reason of the *expression of opinions and standpoints* in accordance with the programme concept and the rules, criteria and standards of the profession (MMA, Article 21).

II. Audio-Visual Media

326. Article 5 of the ARTV stipulates that journalists of RTV Slovenia, in particular, have to respect the principle of *truthfulness, impartiality and integrity* of information, respect the human personality and dignity.

327. Journalists, according to ARTV, have to further respect the principle of *political balance* and *philosophical pluralism* and the principles of *constitutionality and legality* in the design of programmes, including a ban on the promotion of cultural, religious, sexual, racial, ethnic or other forms of intolerance. Journalists are obliged by law to provide *impartial and comprehensive information* so that citizens have the possibility of free formation of opinions.

328. Journalists are obliged by ARTV to respect the principle of political independence and autonomy of journalists, *to promote professional ethics* for reporters and consistent *distinction between information and comments in press charges.*

329. It is explicitly stipulated in the ARTV, that RTV Slovenia is bound to adhere to the principles of impartiality, integrity of information, as well as *journalistic independence and autonomy.*

§3. Protection of Journalistic Sources: Media Law

330. Protection of journalistic sources is explicitly stipulated in Slovenian legislation (MMA). It is laid down by the law (MMA, Article 21), that journalists and the authors/creators are, legally *not obliged to reveal the sources* of their information. The same is true for editorial personnel. The exception of this rule is possible where such is stipulated by criminal legislation.

331. According to Code, the journalist *should identify the source whenever feasible.* Also the journalist should avoid surreptitious methods of gathering information. If information vital to the public cannot be otherwise obtained, the journalist's actions and the reasons for them should be made public and properly explained. The public is entitled to know the source if it is to appraise the significance and credibility of the information. The journalist *may consent to the anonymity* of the source of information cannot be otherwise acquired. The journalist *may decline to testify and disclose his source.* Code stipulates that he journalist should *avoid paying for information* and be wary of sources expecting money or any special privilege in exchange for information.

Chapter 3. Journalists' Liability

§1. Editorial Liability

I. Responsible Editor

332. According to Article 18 of the MMA, each mass medium *must have a responsible editor*, who is appointed and dismissed by the publisher/broadcaster. Before appointing or dismissing the responsible editor the publisher/broadcaster must obtain an *opinion from the editorial board* unless stronger influence on the part of the editorial board is stipulated in the basic legal act (for example consent or veto).

333. The responsible editor is responsible for the implementation of the programme concept and performs other tasks stipulated by the publisher's/broadcaster's basic legal act. The responsible editor is *responsible for any information published* unless stipulated otherwise by the MMA. If a mass medium has *more than one responsible editor*, each is responsible for the publication of information in the programme area for which he/she is responsible (MMA, Article 19).

334. MMA (Article 19) prescribes *condition for the position* of responsible editor; any person who fulfils the following conditions may be a responsible editor:

- the person possesses a certificate of active knowledge of Slovene if the person is not a citizen of the Republic of Slovenia;
- the person possesses a certificate of active knowledge of Hungarian or Italian in the event that the mass medium is for the Hungarian or Italian ethnic communities;
- the person has commercial capability;
- no ban on working in the profession, performing activities or making public appearances has been pronounced against the person.

II. Editorial Board

335. Article 20 of the MMA provides that the editorial board must comprise the responsible editor or *responsible editors, other editorial personnel and journalists*, and in accordance with the publisher's/broadcaster's basic legal act may also comprise other authors/creators of programme pieces and programme collaborators.

336. The legal relations between the publisher/broadcaster and the editorial board and the basic mutual relations within the editorial board must be set out by the *publisher's/broadcaster's basic legal act* in accordance with the MMA, whereby such act must define the editorial board's degree of autonomy in regulating relations within the editorial board.

337. If the *publisher/broadcaster* does not employ several editorial personnel or journalists, the responsible editor may perform the function of the editorial board *alone.*

§2. Defamation and Libel

I. Penal Provisions

338. PC of the Republic of Slovenia[99] in the chapter, titled: Criminal Offences Against Honour and Reputation, incriminates the following criminal actions, that can also be done by press or broadcasting*: insult, defamation, injurious accusation, exposure of personal and family circumstances, reproaching of a criminal offence with the intention to disparage* (Articles 158–162 of the PC). All these criminal actions can be done by press or broadcasting as a qualified manner.[100]

339. Public announcement of all offenses against honour and reputation (including offences done by press or broadcasting) is regulated by Article 166 of the PC. It is stipulated, that *editor (or acting editor) is punished* for the offenses that are committed by the publication of such acts in newspapers and magazines, radio and television programmes, electronic publications, teletext or in other forms of daily or periodic publications or on websites within the limits of the penalties prescribed for the offense; exception is the transfer of live broadcasts as such acts that could not be prevented.

340. The same is the punishment for the *publisher or printer*, if there was a public announcement of the above offenses (Articles 158 to 165 of the Code) committed by non-periodic printed publication, and the manufacturer, if it was committed by recording discs, CD-ROM, film, DVD them and other video sources, audio or similar means, aimed at a broader audience.

341. Special ground for the remission of penalties for offenses referred to in Articles 158 to 162 of the PC is defined in Article 167 of the PC. Namely, if the offender from Article 158 to Article 162 of the PC is provoked by *indecent or brutality of the victim* or *apologies* at the court to the victim, or *revokes what* is claimed or amounted to challenge, the *court may waive the punishment.*

342. There are also some *specific provisions on enforcement* of the offences from Article 168 to Article 162 of the PC. Namely, the prosecution for these offenses must be *initiated upon a private action.* Only if such offenses are committed against

99. Official Gazette of the Republic of Slovenia, no. 55/2008 of 28.5. 2008.
100. The 2009 World Press Freedom index, compiled by Reporters without Borders, a media watchdog, rates most eastern EU members a lot worse this year than in 2008 (see table). Slovenia sharpened its defamation law, extending criminal liability from reporters to publishers and editors. In July prosecutors charged a Finnish journalist who had quoted unnamed sources alleging that Janez Jansa, a former prime minister, took bribes. In August a gagging order was placed on a Slovene newspaper that wrote about an Italian businessman.

governmental authority or municipal or regional authority or against an official or military person in connection with the performance of their service in this body, the prosecution begins on the proposal. If the offenses from Article 168 to Article 162 of the PC are committed against the *deceased person*, the prosecution must be initiated upon a private action by spouse, a person with whom the deceased lived in a consensual union, partner of a registered same-sex partnership, its children or children adopted, parents or adoptive parents, brothers or sisters.

343. There are also special rules for publication of judgment set out by Article 169 of the PC. It is stipulated that in the case of conviction for those offenses committed with the press, radio, television or other means of public communication, the court may at the request of the injured party decide that the *judgment at the expense of the convicted person must be published* in the same way as offense is committed in whole or in extract.

II. Insult

344. Article 158 (Insult) stipulates:

(1) Whoever insults another, shall be punished by a fine or by imprisonment of up to three months.
(2) If the offence under the preceding paragraph has been committed through the press, radio, television or other means of public information or at a public assembly, the perpetrator shall be punished by a fine or by imprisonment of up to six months.

345. Criminal action against insult can be made in a qualified manner *by press or broadcasters*, which are punished more stringently, in effect double (by imprisonment up to six months as compared to up to three months).

346. But there is an important exception that excludes the existence of criminal offence; namely when somebody (whoever) expresses words offensive to another in a scientific, literary or artistic work, in a serious piece of criticism or in the exercise of official duty, *in performing of journalists' profession*, in the course of political or other social activity or in defence of justified benefits; in such a case he or she shall not be punished, provided that the manner of expression or other circumstances indicate that his expression *was not meant to be derogatory* (PC 158/3).

347. In other words, when somebody (whoever) expresses words offensive to another *in performing of journalists' profession*, he or she shall *not be punished*, provided that *the manner of expression* or other circumstances indicate that his expression *was not meant to be derogatory*. If the injured person has returned the insult, the Court may punish both parties or one of them or may remit the punishment (PC 158/4).[101]

III. Defamation

348. Defamation is incriminated in Article 159 of the PC, as follows:

(1) Whoever asserts or circulates anything untruthful about another person which is capable of damaging his honour or reputation and which he knows to be false, shall be punished by a fine or by imprisonment of up to six months.

(2) If the offence under the preceding paragraph has been committed through the press, radio, television or other means of public information or at a public assembly, the perpetrator shall be punished by a fine or by imprisonment of up to one year.

349. There is an important difference between insult and defamation in Slovene penal law. Namely in the case of insult, *the facts are not necessary untruthful* and it is not necessary that the perpetrator knows to be false. In the case of defamation, on the contrary, the facts asserted or circulated about another person *must be untruthful*; if the asserted or circulated facts are the truth, it is not a criminal offense.

350. Paragraph 3 incriminates the qualified way of committing this crime (*grave consequences* for the damaged person); namely if that which has been untruthfully asserted or circulated is of such a nature that it may bring about grave consequences for the damaged person, the perpetrator shall be punished by imprisonment of up to two years.

IV. Injurious Accusation

351. Article 160 of the PC stipulates that whoever asserts or circulates anything about another person which is capable of causing damage to the honour or reputation of that person *no mater, whether it is truth or not* shall be punished by a fine or by imprisonment of up to three months. If this offence has been committed through *the press, radio, television or other means* of public information or at a public assembly, the perpetrator is punished by a fine or by imprisonment up to six months.

101. *See also*: Decision of the Constitutional Court, finding that the third paragraph of Article 169 and the fourth paragraph of Article 171 of the Criminal Code are not inconsistent with the Constitution (Official Gazette of RS, no. 60/1999, 7 of 29 1999).

352. If what has been asserted or circulated is of such a nature that it may *bring about grave consequences* for the defamed person, the perpetrator is punished by a fine of by imprisonment of up to one year.

353. If the perpetrator *proves either the truth* of his assertions or *that he had reasonable grounds* to believe in the truthfulness of what has been asserted or circulated, he shall *not be punished* for injurious accusation but may be punished either for insult (Article 158) or for reproach of a criminal offence with the intention to disparage (Article 162).

354. If whoever asserts or circulates for another *person that he has committed a criminal offence* for which a perpetrator is prosecuted ex officio, then the truthfulness that a damaged person has committed a criminal offence may only be proved by means of a final judgment. Other evidence may be allowed to prove only when prosecution or trial before a Court is not possible or permitted.

355. *As for journalists, there is an important exception.* Namely, if the injurious accusation asserting that the damaged person has committed a criminal offence, for which the perpetrator is prosecuted ex officio, has been committed *in performing of journalists' profession* (third paragraph of Article 158 of the PC), the perpetrator is not punished for injurious accusation even without the existence of a final judgment when he can prove that he had *a justified reason to believe* in the truthfulness of what he had been asserting or circulating.

V. Exposure of Personal and Family Circumstances

356. Exposure of personal and family circumstances as criminal offence is defined in Article 161 of the PC. This criminal offence can be done by whomever who *asserts or circulates any matter concerning the personal or family life* of another person which is capable of injuring that person's reputation; it is punished by a fine or by imprisonment of up to three months.

357. If the offence has been committed through the *press, radio, television or other means* of public information or at a public assembly, the perpetrator is punished by a fine or by imprisonment of up to six months. If what has been asserted or circulated is of such a nature that it brings about *grave consequences* for the damaged person, the perpetrator is punished by a fine or by imprisonment of up to one year.

358. In this case it is *not permitted to prove truthfulness or untruthfulness* of what is asserted or circulated from the personal or family life of another person (except, when action was done in the exercise of official duty, political or other social activity).

359. Only when action was done in the *exercise of official duty, political or other social activity*, the defence of any right or the protection of justified benefits, shall *not be punished*, provided that he *proves either the truthfulness* of his assertions or that he had a reasonable ground for believing in the truthfulness of what has been asserted or circulated.

VI. Reproaching of a Criminal Offence with the Intention to Disparage

360. Article 162 of the PC stipulates that whoever with the intention to disparage reproaches another person that he has committed a criminal offence or has been convicted for the same, or whoever communicates such a fact to a third person with the same intention shall be punished by a fine or by imprisonment of up to three months.

361. If such an offence has been committed through the *press, radio, television or other means* of public information or at a public assembly, the perpetrator shall be punished by a fine or by imprisonment of up to six months.

VII. Tort Liability – Libel and Slander

362. Defamation, libel and slander are *civil wrongs* that harm a reputation, decrease respect, regard, or confidence; or induce disparaging, hostile, or disagreeable opinions or feelings against an individual or entity. The injury to one's good name or reputation is affected through written or spoken words or visual images.[102]

363. In Slovenian Code on Obligations (hereinafter Obligations Code or CO)[103] lays down the rules on reimbursement material or/immaterial damage, caused by defamation or calumny.

364. In case of *material damage* caused by defamation or calumny, person that defames another or asserts or disseminates *untrue statements* (or the person that defames knows or should have known that they were untrue) on the past, knowledge or capability of another, must reimburse such damage.

365. I*mmaterial damage* pertains to the injured party for physical and mental distress suffered owing to the defamation of good name or reputation even if there was no material damage. But it is necessary to add, that immaterial damage pertains only if the circumstances of the case, particularly the level and duration of distress and fear, so justify.

102. *See also*: http://legal-dictionary.thefreedictionary.com/Libel+and+Slander.
103. Code of Obligations (consolidated text) / OZ-UPB1 / Official RS, no. 97/2007.

VIII. General on Damage Liability under CO

366. CO sets out legal basis for damage liability is set out in in the provision, that any person that inflicts damage on another is obliged to reimburse it, unless it is proved that the damage was incurred without the culpability of the former (paragraph one of the Article 131 of the CO). For damages regardless of guilt one could be liable in cases stipulated by law.

367. Guilt is given when the infringing party has caused damage deliberately or through negligence.

368. CO in the Article 132 defines the term 'damage'; it stipulates, that damage comprises the diminution of property (ordinary damage), prevention of the appreciation of property (lost profits), the infliction of *physical or mental distress or fear* on another person, and *encroachment upon the reputation* of a person. Damage can though be *material or/and immaterial.*

IX. Reimbursement of Material Damage in Case of Defamation or Calumny

369. Reimbursement of material damage in case of defamation or calumny is set out in the Article 177 of the CO. It is stipulated there, that any *person that defames* another or asserts or disseminates *untrue statements* on the past, knowledge or capability of another, even though the former *knows or should have known* that they were untrue, and thereby inflicts material damage on the latter, must reimburse such damage. The statements should therefore be untrue or the *person that defames* knows *or should have known* that they were untrue.

370. However any person that reports anything untrue about another without knowing that such was untrue is not be liable for the damage inflicted if there is a genuine interest in so doing for the former or the person to whom the report was made.

371. Any how the material *damage must be inflicted*; otherwise, there is no damage liability.

X. Reimbursement of Immaterial Damage

372. Article 179 of the CO sets out *monetary compensation*. It says that just monetary compensation independent of the reimbursement of immaterial damage pertains to the injured party for *physical distress* suffered, for *mental distress* suffered owing to the *defamation of good name or reputation*, if the circumstances of the case, particularly the level and duration of distress and fear, so justify, *even if there was no material damage*.

373. The amount of compensation for immaterial damage depends on the *importance of the good affected* and the purpose of the compensation, and may not support tendencies that are not compatible with the nature and purpose thereof.

374. The court awards a legal person just monetary *compensation for the defamation* of reputation or good name, *independent of the reimbursement of material damage*, if it finds that the circumstances so justify, even if there is no material damage (Article 183 of the CO).

375. According to Article 184 of the CO, the claim for the reimbursement of immaterial damage *passes to heirs* only if it was recognized by a final legal ruling or a written agreement. Such a claim may be the subject of assignment, offset and execution under equal conditions.

XI. Publication of Judgment

376. Article 178 of the CO regulates the *publication of judgment* or correction. In a case of the infringement of a personal right the court may order the publication of the judgment or a correction at the injurer's expense or order that the injurer must retract the statement by which the infringement was committed or do anything else through which it is possible to achieve the purpose achieved via compensation.

§3. Privacy

I. Personal Data Protection Act

377. Slovenian PDPA (Slov.: Zakon o varstvu osebnih podatkov, ZVOP-1)[104] determines the rights, responsibilities, principles and measures to prevent unconstitutional, unlawful and unjustified encroachments on the privacy and dignity of an individual in the processing of personal data.

378. The law is based upon principle of lawfulness and fairness, principle of proportionality, and prohibition of discrimination.

II. Personal Data Breach

379. Personal data breach, according to ECA means a breach of security leading to the accidental or unlawful destruction, loss, alteration, unauthorized disclosure of or access to personal data transmitted, retained or otherwise processed in connection with the provision of a publicly available electronic communications service in the EU.

104. Official Gazette of the Republic of Slovenia, No. 86/2004, as of 5 Aug. 2004, as amended by 113/2005-ZInfP, 51/2007-ZUstS-A, 67/2007, 94/2007-UPB1 (official consolidated text).

380. The rights, responsibilities, principles and measures to prevent unconstitutional, unlawful and unjustified encroachments on the privacy and dignity of an individual in the processing of personal data are more precisely defined by the PDPA.

III. Processing of Personal Data

381. Processing of personal data, according to law (Article 6 of the PDPA) means any operation or set of operations performed in connection with personal data that are subject to processing which are intended for inclusion in particular collection, acquisition, recording, organization, storage, adaptation or alteration, retrieval, consultation, use, disclosure by transmission, communication, dissemination or otherwise making available, alignment or linking, blocking, anonymizing, erasure or destruction. Processing may be performed *manually or by using automated technology* (means of processing).

382. PDPA does not apply to the processing of personal data performed by individuals exclusively for personal use, family life or for other domestic needs. Articles 26, 27 and 28 of PDPA, regulating notification *of filing systems do* not apply to personal data, which are processed by political parties, trade unions, associations or religious communities relating to their members.

383. The second paragraph of Articles 26, 27 and 28, of PDPA, regulating notification of filing systems and Part V of this PDPA, regulating rights of the individual do not apply to personal data which are processed by the media for the purposes of informing the public.

IV. Rights of Individuals Referring to Data Protection

384. The following rights are guaranteed to individual referring to his or her personal data:

- *Right of the individual to information; this* right corresponds to the duty of the data controller to enable consultation of the filing system catalogue, to certify whether data relating to individual are being processed or not, and to enable him to consult personal data contained in filing system that relate to him, and to transcribe or copy them and several other duties.
- *Right to supplement, correct, block, erase and to object*; on the request of an individual to whom personal data relate, the data controller must supplement, correct, block or erase personal data which the individual proves as being incomplete, inaccurate or not up to date, or that they were collected or processed contrary to statute.
- *Right to judicial protection of the rights of the individual;* individual who finds that his rights provided by PDPA (Article 34) have been violated may request

judicial protection for as long as such violation lasts. The competent court decides in the procedure under the provisions of the statute regulating administrative disputes.

V. Restriction of the Rights of an Individual

385. Restriction of the rights of an individual are possible in the cases referred to in the Article 36 of the PDPA, as for reasons of protection of national sovereignty and national defence, protection of national security and the Constitutional order of the state, security, political and economic interests of the state, the exercise of the responsibilities of the police, the prevention, discovery, detection, proving and prosecution of criminal offences and minor offences, the discovery and punishment of violations of ethical norms for certain professions, for monetary, budgetary or tax reasons, supervision of the police, and protection of the individual to whom the personal data relate, or the rights and freedoms of others.

Chapter 4. Right to Correction and Right to Reply

§1. General on Right to Correct and Right to Reply

386. The right to *correct* published information which has damaged a right or interest of an individual, organization or body is guaranteed, as it is the right to *reply* to such published information (Article 40 of the Constitution of Slovenia).

387. Both rights (Correction and Reply) are in details elaborated in the respective Law on Mass Media.[105] Legal regulation of both rights (Correction and Reply) refer to all media (printed and broadcasting).

§2. Right to Correction

388. According to Slovenian Law, any person has the right to demand that the responsible editor publish free of charge a *correction* by such person to any information published that infringed upon the person's rights or interests The publication of a correction may be requested within thirty days of the date on which the interested party had learned to publish the notice, but not later than three months after the publication of the notice (amended Article 26 of the MMA).

389. According to Article 27 of the MMA, the correction must be published *without substantive amendments or supplements.* Only spelling corrections are allowed, provided that the person affected had been informed of and *agreed* to them.

390. The correction must be published in such *form and place* that its publication has the same value as the article or the contribution to which it refers.

391. If a correction refers to two or more notices covering the same event or the same person and having been published in different media of the same publisher/ broadcaster, the correction must be published in all those media.

§3. Right to Reply to Information Published

392. It is stipulated by the MMA, that any person has the right to demand that the responsible editor *publish free of charge a reply to information* published by which that person through demonstrable statements denies, significantly corrects or significantly elaborates upon the statement of facts and figures in the information published.

105. *See* on detailed elaboration in the Chapter Freedom of Expression of this book.

393. Replies must be, according to Article 43 of the MMA, published *without substantive amendments* or additions, with the exception of grammatical corrections. The responsible editor has the right to request prior to publication an abridgement of the reply by the author.

394. The provisions on the legal grounds for rejection of the publication of correction (Article 31) of the MMA applies to a reply, whereby the responsible editor may reject the publication of replies of the same content when a single reply has already been published. The responsible editor may also reject the publication of a reply if the reply cites untrue or indemonstrable information or assertions.

§4. The Right to File a Suit Against the Responsible Editor

395. If the responsible editor fails to publish a correction or reply within the defined period and in the manner stipulated by MMA the person that demanded the publication of the correction has according to the Article 33 of the MMA *the* right to *file a suit against the responsible editor.*

396. The court *competent court is* the court for civil disputes in the area of the head office or permanent residence of the publisher/broadcaster of the mass medium through which the report to which the correction relates was published. A suit may be filed within thirty days of the expiry of the deadline for publishing the correction, or of the day on which the correction was published in a manner not in accordance with the MMA.

Chapter 5. Access to Public Information

§1. Access to Public Information

I. Public Information

397. The *APIA*[106] adopted in Slovenian Parliament in 2003 governs the procedure which ensures everyone free access to and reuse of public information held by state bodies, local government bodies, public agencies, public funds and other entities of public law, public powers holders and public service contractors (the bodies).

398. The aim of APIA is to ensure that the work of the bodies is public and open and to enable natural and legal entities to exercise their right to acquire information held by public authorities (Articles 1 and 2 of the APIA).

399. According to Article 4 of the APIA, public information is deemed to be information originating from the field of work of the body and occurring in the form of a document, a case, a dossier, a register, a record or other documentary material (the document) drawn up by the body, by the body in cooperation with other body, or acquired from other persons.

400. Archive material held by the competent Archive, within the frame of public archive service in accordance with the Act governing archives, is not public information according to APIA.

II. Free Access Principle

401. According to APIA (Article 5), legal entities or natural persons (the applicants) have free access to public information. Each applicant has, at his request, *the right to acquire information* from the body by acquiring such information for consulting it on the spot, or by acquiring a transcript, a copy or an electronic record of such information.

402. Every applicant has the right, under the same conditions as all other persons, to acquire the right to reuse the information for commercial or non-commercial purposes.

403. The body makes its public information *available through electronic means* where possible and appropriate though this does not imply an obligation, for the purpose of the reuse of information, to provide transformation of one form into

106. Access to Public Information Act (APIA, official consolidated version (Zakon o dostopu do informacij javnega značaja, UPB2, Official Gazette of the Republic of Slovenia, No. 51/06).

other or provide extracts from documents, where this would involve disproportionate effort, going beyond a simple operation, nor continue with the provision of certain information only for the purpose of reuse by other bodies or other persons.

III. Exceptions

404. There are of course several exceptions to the free access principle (APIA, Article 5a). The applicant authority shall refuse access to the requested information or reuse it if the request relates to information in respect of which *access under the law is prohibited or limited* to parties, participants or victims in judicial, administrative or law-specified control procedure (APIA, Article 5a).

405. There are several other reasons for exceptions stipulated by APIA that draw a sharp and clear line between the information that is publicly accessible and the ones that are exceptionally not.

The applicant authority shall refuse access to the requested information or reuse it if the request relates to information obtained or drawn up in the light of a *supervisory procedure, which is managed by Banka Slovenije* under the law, by the authority responsible for the surveillance of the *market securities or insurance supervision*, or by another supervisory body, specializing in financial supervision if the control procedure is still underway. When the control procedure is completed, the authority may refuse access to or reuse it even if disclosure of the requested information would cause harm to another person or if it would seriously undermine the implementation of other statutory tasks of the control institution, which led the procedure. The applicant authority shall refuse access to the requested information or reuse it if the request relates to the information in respect of which the law provides for the protection of the secrecy of the source (APIA, Article 5a).

§2. Duties of All Bodies

406. All the bodies, like *state bodies, local government bodies, public agencies, public funds* and other entities of public law, public powers holders and public service contractors are obliged to maintain the so-called catalogue of public information and appoint one or more officials competent for the communication of public information. In addition, each of them is obliged to transmit to the World Wide Web public information, listed exactly in the Law.

407. The applicant *may request access to public information* by way of written request for access to or the reuse of public information, or by way of an informal request. Both procedures are precisely regulated by the Law and relevant sub laws. The body may refuse the applicant's request, in whole or in part, if it finds the requested data or document to be exempt under Article 6 of this APIA.

408. There is a *right of appeal against the decision* by which the body has refused the request, as well as against the order by which the body has dismissed the request. The Commissioner for Access to Public Information decides on the appeal.

409. Appellate proceeding is implemented in accordance with the provisions laid down in the Act governing the *general administrative procedure*. An administrative dispute may be started against the decision by the Commissioner.

410. The state bodies and the local government bodies are obliged to draw up an *annual report* on the implementation of APIA and submit it to the Ministry by 31 January for the previous year.

411. The government draws up a *joint annual report* on the implementation of APIA, based on the received reports and submit it to the National Assembly of the Republic of Slovenia into reading.

Part III. Regulation of Audiovisual Media (Broadcasting)

Chapter 1. Public Service Broadcasting

§1. The Concept and Mission of Public Service Broadcasting

I. The Public Interest in the Area of the Mass Media

412. As declared in the Article 4 of the MMA, the Republic of Slovenia supports the mass media in the creation and dissemination of programme important to the exercise of *the right of citizens* of the Republic of Slovenia, *to public information* and *to be informed in general.* The same right belongs equally to Slovenes around the world, members of the Slovene minorities, ethnic communities in Slovenia, and the Romani community living in Slovenia.

413. The Republic of Slovenia provides for the funds needed for co-financing the exercising of the public interest in the field of the mass media in the *state budget* (Article 4 of the MMA). The Republic of Slovenia extra supports the development of *technical infrastructure* in the area of the broadcasting media.

II. RTV Slovenia as an Independent Entity of Special Cultural and National Importance

414. ARTV regulates the status and operation of the Radio and Television Corporation of Slovenia (Slov.: Radiotelevizija Slovenija, hereinafter RTV Slovenia). RTV Slovenia is an *independent legal person of special cultural and national importance* governed by public law. Within the performance of public service laid down by the Act, RTV Slovenia provides a wide range of contents, programmes and services, without discrimination and on the basis of equal opportunities, through various transmission paths.

415. The objective of RTV Slovenia as laid down by the ARTV is to *fulfil the democratic, social and cultural needs* of the inhabitants of the Republic of Slovenia, citizens of the Republic of Slovenia and of Slovenians living abroad and autochthonous Italian and Hungarian national communities. At the same time, the law stipulates that RTV Slovenia covers Roma community, members of national communities of the former Yugoslav republics and members of other national and ethnic communities in the Republic of Slovenia.

416. RTV Slovenia is legally obliged to ensuring *pluralism, including cultural and linguistic diversity,* and other activities in accordance with the law. RTV Slovenia has to provide the public with the benefits of new audio-visual and information services and new technologies and follow development.

417. The only founder and owner of RTV Slovenia is the Republic of Slovenia. The duty of the *founder is to ensure the professional and editorial independence* of RTV Slovenia, appropriate financing and suitable arrangement which serves as the basis to obtain funds for the provision of public service while respecting the financial stability of RTV Slovenia's funding sources.

III. Special Programme Services

418. MMA stipulates, that the Republic of Slovenia supports the activities of Radio Television of Slovenia, *local, regional, student and non-profit* radio and television programme services that are of special importance to Slovenian culture using funds from the national budget (Decision of the Constitutional Court – repealed (Official Gazette of the RS, No. 16-648/2004) (Article 82 of the MMA).

419. Three percent of RTV licence fee funds are set aside for preparing the programme of *local, regional and student radio and television programme services.* Funds are provided from the national budget for the construction, maintenance and operation of the broadcast and transmission network for the dissemination of local, regional, student and non-profit radio and television programme services.

420. For *special* programme services, the collective organization of authors/creators set a special tariff reduced by up to 20% for the use of works under copyright, in accordance with the act regulating the protection of copyright and related rights.

421. Detailed criteria for the definition and financing of *local, regional, informative, cultural, educational, entertainment* and other programme specified in the present Act are set out by the relevant ministry at the proposal of the Broadcasting Council). At the proposal of the Broadcasting Council, the relevant ministry adopts implementing regulations in which the procedure and conditions for acquiring or revoking the *status of special programme* services are set out in detail in accordance (Article 82/6 of the MMA).

IV. In-House Production

422. Article 67 of the MMA stipulates that *informative arts and culture, educational, entertainment* and phone-in programmes, musical, sports and other programmes with commentary and other original programme produced by the broadcaster of the programme service or produced under commission from and at the expense of the broadcaster are *deemed programme created in in-house production.*

423. If several broadcasters participate in the production of the programme via investments, the proportion of the investment is deemed the proportion of in-house production for each broadcaster.

424. The presentation of *Slovenian music* also counts towards the quota of in-house production of a *radio* programme service. Under the MMA 'Slovenian music' is the music of Slovene origin, which covers the concepts of vocal, vocal-instrumental and instrumental music. Advertisements, including radio-sales and telesales, and unpaid reports (teletext) are *not deemed* programme created in in-house production.

425. The relevant ministry must via implementing regulations set out *detailed criteria* for the definition of the programme specified in this article at the proposal of the Broadcasting Council.

V. Slovenian Audio-Visual Works

426. Slovenian audio-visual works are *works produced originally in Slovene* or works intended for the Hungarian and Italian ethnic communities in the language thereof, and *works of Slovenian cultural origin* from other areas of the arts Slovenian Audio-visual works are only those expressed in any manner as individual intellectual creations from the fields of literature, science and art.

427. The Republic of Slovenia supports the establishment and progressive development of the *Slovenian audio-visual industry* and promotes the creation of Slovenian audio-visual works, such as TV feature films and dramas, arts and culture series, entertainment series, serials, documentaries and educational works. The Republic of Slovenia also promotes the development of technical infrastructure for audio-visual production (MMA, Article 68).

§2. HISTORY AND EVOLUTION

I. History of Radio

428. Radio Ljubljana signed on the air for the first time on *1 September 1928*, with experimental broadcasts. By October 28 the radio station already had a scheduled program. On 11 April 1941, the station's transmitter in Domžale was destroyed, and the station was occupied by Italian Fascists.[107]

429. Second radio programme started in *1951*.

430. In 2008 RTV Slovenia celebrated the *80th anniversary of Radio Slovenia* (its forerunner Radio Ljubljana was established in 1928) and the 50th anniversary of Televizija Slovenija (regular television broadcasting commenced in 1958).

II. History of Television

431. In *1929* the inventor Codelli from Ljubljana *transmitted this private image* with the help of the technology of photography and the cable transmission.

432. On *1 April 1949, the first TV laboratory* was established in Ljubljana but was separate from the radio station. However, the task of setting-up a television service was eventually assigned to Radio Ljubljana. On 11 November 1958, the TV channel got a regular schedule, but it was shared by other Yugoslav republics, with TV Ljubljana getting around 30% of airtime.

433. In *1971, TV Koper/Capodistria,* a subsidiary of RTV Ljubljana, was launched as the first bilingual TV station in Slovenia, serving the Italian community in Slovenia and Croatia. During the 1970s, TV Ljubljana's main service was also gradually converted to colour. In 1984, teletext was introduced, whereas the digitalization started in 1986. In 1989, Radio Ljubljana started transmitting an RDS signal.

434. A year before Slovenia's independence in *1991, the institution was renamed* to Radiotelevizija Slovenija (from RTV Ljubljana). On 1 January 1993, RTV Slovenija was admitted as a fully active member of the European Broadcasting Union following the collapse of Yugoslavia, and began participation in the Eurovision Song Contest.

435. In the mid- to late 1990s, TV Slovenia began to face increased competition from Slovenia's commercial television stations. In 1995, RTV Slovenia published its first web page. Radio *digitalization started in 1995*, whereas the digitalization of television broadcasting started in 1999.

107. *See*: http://www.culture.si/en/Radio-Television_Slovenia_(RTV_Slovenia).

436. In *1997, satellite broadcasting* started via Hot Bird 3. In 2001, RTV Slovenija's Multimedia Centre was established to help introduce new technologies. A new multimedia web portal was introduced in 2002.

437. In May 2008 TV Slovenia began airing a new TV channel, *TV Slovenija 3*, dedicated primarily to live Parliament coverage. In 2011, the analogue signal was abandoned.[2

§3. MISSION

438. The mission of media could be explained by the definition of *public interest* in the field of media in the RS. According to the Resolution on the National Programme for Culture 2014–2017,[108] the implementation of the *Constitutional right to freedom of expression*, including the *right to public information* is in public interest. Likewise, cultural, ideological and geographical *pluralism and diversity of media* content, the development of the Slovenian national and *cultural identity* and the Slovenian *language* and care for their visibility, the consolidation of *social values* such as basic *human rights, democracy and tolerance* (including the importance which both *social inclusion and intergenerational cooperation* for the healthy development of the company) is also in public interest.

439. The autonomy of the journalistic profession, *transparency* of media ownership, *equity pluralism* and *prevention of abuse* of a dominant position in the media market is in public interest.

440. And, not least, increasing the availability of media content for *vulnerable social groups* and disabled handicapped, the existence of television and radio programmes of special interest (assuming to re- determine their importance, role, status and financing) is also public interest.[109]

441. As for the media field, public interest is the promotion and development of *media literacy*, the production of *high-quality media content* in the areas of arts and culture, critical reflection of society, education, science, the environment, etc., the production of high-quality media *content for children and adolescents*, the promotion of *investigative journalism*, demanding and *specific journalistic genres* and content, improving the social *status of independent and young journalists* and the emergence of *new forms of media ownership* – management models.[110]

108. Ministry of Culture, the Resolution on the National Program for Culture 2014–2017.
109. *Ibid.*
110. *Ibid.*

§4. The Organization of Public Service Broadcasting

I. The Public Institution RTV Slovenia

442. Public service of producing and disseminating radio and television programme services in the public and cultural interest of the Republic of Slovenia is *carried out by the public institution RTV Slovenia* (Article 76 of the MMA). Public service in this field includes radio and television programme services of the Italian and Hungarian ethnic communities and other programme services in accordance with ARTV.

443. According to Article 3 of the ARTV, *public service* comprises the creating, producing, archiving and broadcasting of:

- two national television channels;
- three national radio channels;
- radio and television channels at regional centres in Koper and Maribor;
- one radio and television channel each for the autochthonous Italian and Hungarian ethnic communities and radio and television broadcasts for the Roma ethnic community, radio and television channels for Slovenian ethnic minorities in neighbouring countries and for Slovenian expatriates and migrant workers;
- radio and television channels for the foreign public;
- teletext, internet and mobile portals.

444. Public interest in addition, comprise a *special national television channel* intended to provide live transmission of sessions of the National Assembly of the Republic of Slovenia and its working bodies, and broadcasting of recordings of such sessions where live transmission is not possible, including sessions of the National Council of the Republic of Slovenia, the international activities and other activities associated with the exercising of Constitutional powers by the Slovenian Parliament and National Council.

445. The founding rights in connection with the operation of the public institution RTV Slovenia are exercised by the *government* via the relevant *ministry (of culture)*, except insofar as a separate act sets out individual founding rights and obligations for the RTV Slovenia Council or the National Assembly of the Republic of Slovenia.

446. The name of the public institution is in Slovene: Radiotelevizija Slovenija (Public institution The Radio and Television of Slovenia), abbreviated to RTV Slovenia. The registered office of RTV Slovenia is in Ljubljana.

II. Local Radio and Television Programme Services

447. According to Article 77 of the MMA, programme service that covers, with the low-lying terrestrial broadcasting, the area of *one or more local communities* or an area of coverage in which no more than 10% of the population of the Republic of Slovenia live, and that carries local programme produced in-house for *at least 20%* of its transmission time between 6 a.m. and 8 p.m. is considered a local radio programme service.

448. A programme service that covers, with the low-lying terrestrial broadcasting, the area of one or more local communities or an area of coverage in which *no more than 10% of the population* of the Republic of Slovenia live, and that carries local programme produced in-house for at least 20% of its transmission time between 8 a.m. and midnight is considered a *local television programme service.* The minimum transmission time of a local television programme service is three hours per day and four (4) days per week (Article 77 of the MMA).

449. In exceptional cases a programme service that does not achieve the proportion of local programme produced in-house may acquire the status of a local radio or television programme service if such a programme service is disseminated in a *demographically disadvantaged* or *economically undeveloped area,* and there is no other local radio or television programme service in the area, provided that the broadcaster also meets the conditions (Article 77 of the MMA).

450. According to Article 78 of the MMA, a broadcaster may acquire the status of a *local radio or television* programme service if it also fulfils the following extra conditions:

- the programme service provides objective and unbiased *information for inhabitants* of the local community and the balanced presentation of different opinions and views on political, cultural, religious, economic and other issues important to the life and work of the local inhabitants;
- the broadcaster appoints a *programme committee* in which the interests of the local community in the areas of commerce, culture, education and sport, and of the broadcaster of the programme service are represented;
- the programme is primarily of a *local character* and is jointly created by inhabitants of the local community;
- it has a programme from the lives and work of Slovenes in neighbouring countries, members of the *Hungarian and Italian* ethnic communities, and Roma if it is receivable in areas where such communities live;
- the programme service's daily transmission time provides a higher proportion of programme of a local character than other radio and television programme services that fulfil the criteria specified in this article and broadcast in the same area;
- the broadcaster asking that its programme service be given a special status may not broadcast other programmes in the scope of its activity; if other programmes are broadcasted as well, all such programmes must fulfil the conditions required for obtaining such status;
- only the broadcasters that employ at least three people under a permanent employment contract, full-time, may apply for the special status of a local radio and television programme service, and the broadcasters that employ at least six

people under a permanent employment contract, full-time, may apply for the special status of a regional or non-profit radio and television programme service.

451. The *programme committee*, which must have at least three members, monitors the implementation of the programme concept, acquaint the responsible editor with its viewpoints and suggestions, offer opinions on the programme concept and perform other tasks in accordance with the law and the act on the founding of the programme committee. Within fifteen days of adopting the act on the founding of the programme committee or amendments or additions thereto the broadcaster must send such to the Agency for their information (Article 78 of the MMA).

III. Regional Radio and Television Programme Services

452. Article 79 of the MMA considers a regional radio or television programme service the programme service intended for the *inhabitants of an area* (region or town) in which more than 10% and no more than 50% of the population of the Republic of Slovenia live and that carries regional programme produced in-house for at least 30% of its transmission time between 6 a.m. and 8 p.m. if a radio programme service or for at least 30% of its transmission time between 8 a.m. and 12 a.m. The minimum transmission time of a regional television programme service is *five hours per day*, and it must broadcast every day. The conditions for acquiring the status of a regional television programme service and to the performance of the activities thereof are the same as for the local radio and television.

IV. Student Radio and Television Programme Services

453. A student organization may, according to *Article 80 of the MMA,* be the broadcaster of a radio and/or television programme service if the majority of the programme is created and disseminated by students and is primarily aimed at a student audience, and if the surplus of revenues over expenditure is used only for executing the activities for which it was founded, in accordance with the act governing the operation and activities of students' self-managed communities in Slovenia and its basic legal act.

454. The programme of student radio and television programme services comprises information of *all types and works* under copyright whose purpose is providing information and satisfying the educational, scientific, professional, artistic, cultural and other needs of students and the general public.

§5. THE FINANCING OF PUBLIC SERVICE BROADCASTING

I. Financing the Programmes of the Mass Media

455. Article 4a of the MMA regulates the issue of *financing the programmes of the mass media;* it stipulates, that *t*he Republic of Slovenia provides for the budgetary funds for the mass media for the implementation of the *state aid in exercising the public interest* in the mass media within the ministry responsible for culture with the aim of assuring *plurality and democracy of the mass media and the freedom of speech* in the Republic of Slovenia.

456. The Republic of Slovenia provides the funds for *plurality and democracy* of the programme of radio and television programme services and electronic publications and for the development and co-financing of the programme of radio and television programme services with the status of a local, regional or student radio or television programme service or a non-profit radio or television programme service.

457. The amount corresponding *to 3% of the RTV Slovenia* licence fee, collected in the previous year, is allocated to the development of the programme of radio and television programme services with the status of a *local, regional or student* radio or television programme service or a non-profit radio or television programme service. The funds obtained by the broadcaster through the tenders of the competent ministry on the basis of such special status can only be spent for the purposes stated in the MMA.

II. Co-financing Criteria for Radio and Television Programme

458. When discussing the co-financing of the programme of *radio and television programme* services and electronic publications, the following criteria must be observed by the expert committee (Article 4a/9 MMA):

- assuring regular, objective and balanced presentations of the political activities and positions of various organizations and individuals, especially the political coalition and opposition;
- quality, originality, communication and topicality of author's treatment;
- significance of the project for the promotion of the Slovenian culture and language;
- significance of the implementation of the proposed programme aimed at assuring a diversified development of the Slovenian media sphere;
- significance for the protection of the Slovenian national and cultural identity;
- the significance for the exercising of the right to public information and to be informed objectively;
- assuring more jobs or employment relationships for the journalists or the programme staff who help create the medium.

III. Co-financing Criteria for Local, Regional or Student Radio and Television Programme

459. When discussing the co-financing of radio and television programme services with the status of a *local, regional or student* radio or television programme service or a non-profit radio or television programme service, the following criteria must be observed by the expert committee (Article 4a/11 MMA):

- assuring regular, objective and balanced presentations of the political activities and positions of various organizations and individuals, especially the political coalition and opposition;
- quality, originality, communication and topicality of author's treatment;
- the significance of a project for the development of a region, a local community or special contents;
- significance of the implementation of the proposed programme aimed at assuring a diversified development of the Slovene media sphere;
- the significance for the exercising of the right to public information and to be informed objectively;
- non-profitability of a programme as a priority criterion;
- assuring more jobs or employment relationships for the journalists or the programme staff who help create the medium;
- enabling the exercising of the right to public information for the local communities and minorities and whether it is disseminated in the language of such minority;
- assuring compliance with the principle of cultural diversity, the principle of equal opportunities of sexes and tolerance.

460. The competent ministry performs the expert administrative and technical administrative tasks in the area of auditing and assessing the projects for the expert committee.

Chapter 2. Private Broadcasting

§1. Different Categories of Private Broadcasters

I. Broadcaster

461. A broadcaster is a *legal or natural person* that carries out activities of disseminating programme in accordance with MMA. A broadcaster independently formulates the mass medium's *programme concept* and bears fundamental *responsibility* for the implementation thereof. The activities of a broadcaster may also encompass the creation or *production of the programme* (MMA, Article 9).

462. There are special conditions for founding and entering a broadcaster in the court register (MMA, Article 10). In order to carry out activities of disseminating programme a legal or natural person may be founded or *entered in the court register* in the Republic of Slovenia The condition to register is that the person's head office or address of permanent residence is located in the Republic of Slovenia and that the editorial board is based in the Republic of Slovenia.

II. Mass Media Register

463. For the purpose of entry in the *mass media register,* the broadcaster must register the mass medium at the relevant *ministry* prior to commencing the performance of activities. The dates to be filed with the register are the same as prescribed for print media (the *name* of the mass medium, the name of the broadcaster the *address* of editorial board, the name of the *responsible officer*, and of the responsible editor, the type of mass medium and *interval of its dissemination, the method and envisaged area* of coverage and the language of dissemination of programme and the sources and method of *financing and information on persons that hold ownership* or management stakes of at least 5% or stakes of at least 5% in the voting rights within the assets of a broadcaster).

464. Prior to the beginning of transmission broadcasters of a radio or television programme service must submit copies of the *contracts concluded with collective organizations for the protection of copyright* and related rights on works that will be broadcast on their programme services. Broadcasters may *not register* a mass medium that would have the *same name* as a mass medium already entered in the register. By the end of March each year broadcasters of a radio or television programme service must send a *written report* on the performance of activities and the implementation of the programme concept to the respective Agency (MMA, Article 10).

III. Non-profit Radio and Television Programme Services

465. Non-profit programme services are, according to Article 81 of the MMA, the *Radio* programme services that carry informative, arts, educational and cultural entertainment programme produced in-house for at least 30% of their daily transmission time and *television* programme services that carry the programme specified in Article 81 MMA, for at least 30% of their daily transmission time shall be considered.

466. The surplus of revenues over expenditure, i.e. the profit, from the activities may be used by the broadcaster *only for performing radio or television activities*, in accordance with the broadcaster's basic legal act. Employees' pay, the bonuses for members of the broadcaster's management and supervisory bodies and other benefits (travel expenses, daily expenses, etc.) may not exceed the tariff stipulated for public institutions by current regulations and the collective agreement for employees in the area of culture.

467. The low-lying terrestrial broadcasting that does not reach *more than 30%* of the population of the Republic of Slovenia can be issued the non-profit status provided that they fulfil the programme requirements defined by MMA. A programme service that has already obtained the special status of local or regional significance can obtain non-profit status.

468. The broadcaster asking that its programme service be given the special *non-profit* status may *not broadcast other* profit-generating programmes in the scope of its activity.

IV. Radio and Television Networks

469. The broadcasters of television channels that do not have the status of a station of special importance can *link together in terms of programming into regional or national* networks. A national network must reach *more than 50%* of the population of the Republic of Slovenia. Article 83 of the MMA stipulates that publishers of radio and television programme services (with the exception of a special programme service) may *link together* in terms of *the* programme to form wider, *regional or national networks*, with regional or wider coverage of an area.[111]

470. Conditions for linking in terms of programming into networks are the following:

– each of the linked broadcasters in the area for which they received a broadcasting license must broadcast *at least 2 hours of in-house production* daily;

111. *See*: http://www.akos-rs.si/television-networks.

- joint in-house production of linked broadcasters created in Slovenian, and which does not include programming from the previous point, must encompass *at least 25% of the programming content* distributed over the network daily;
- each of the linked broadcasters must *obtain the prior consent of the Agency* if linking into the network would significantly alter their programming content;
- linked broadcasters prepare *joint programming and a written legal act* on the method of its execution, and send both documents to the applicable ministry to be entered into the mass media register;
- the linked broadcasters *appoint the editor in chief* of the joint programming with a special act, and that person is responsible for broadcasting programming content, and the act on appointment is sent to the applicable ministry 15 days before the network begins operations.

471. The television network *does not have its own license*, but its characteristics are instead entered in the licenses of the individual television channels linked in the network. Because this is not an independent television station, it cannot apply to public tenders; however the stations linked in the network can.

§2. Licensing Requirements

I. The Licensing Regime

472. The licensing regime of linear services, after the adoption of AVMSA in 2011, *remains almost unchanged*, as it is defined by the MMA. The difference is that the obligation to get a licence *prior to the start of broadcasting* now applies to all linear AVMS, regardless of the platform. The extension of the licensing regime therefore affects mainly providers of internet television, as they were exempt from it under the previous regulation.[112]

II. Public Tenders for Allocating Radio Frequencies

473. A broadcaster must acquire a decision on allocation of radio frequencies for broadcasting in order to disseminate radio programming via radio frequencies. The decision is issued by the *Agency based on a public tender.*[113]

474. The public tender is initiated by a decision issued by the Agency in agreement with the *Broadcasting Council*. The decision on initiating a public tender is

112. Tanja Kerševan Smokvina, Post and Electronic Communications Agency of the Republic of Slovenia (APEK), Act Transposing the Audio-visual Media Services Directive Adopted: On 19 Oct. 2011, the Act on Audio-visual Media Services (Zakon o avdiovizualnih medijskih storitvah - ZAvMS) was adopted and entered into force on 17 Nov. 2011.

113. *See*: http://www.akos-rs.si/how-the-public-tenders-for-allocating-radio-frequencies-are-conducted.

published in the Official Gazette of the Republic of Slovenia and on the Agency's website. Tender documentation and related forms are published on the Agency's website.

475. The tender documentation provides a *more detailed explanation of the conditions* and criteria by which the bids will be evaluated. The Agency is responsible for assessing some of the criteria, while the criteria regarding programming content are evaluated by the Broadcasting Council.

476. The deadline for submitting the bids is usually 60 days from the day the decision was published in the Official Gazette of the Republic of Slovenia, and the bids should be sent to the Agency's address. After the deadline expires, the commission conducting the public tender opens all bids that arrived on time and were correctly labelled at a public opening.

477. After the public opening, the commission verifies whether individual bids and all related documents meet the requirements from legislation and the tender documentation. It also checks whether the bidder fulfils the criteria from the decision or tender documentation. After that, the bids are assessed by the criteria from the tender documentation.

III. Obtaining Radio Frequencies for Analogue Broadcasting

478. Article 104 of the MMA stipulates the conditions and *criteria for the selection* between the interested providers of the programme for obtaining radio frequencies for analogue broadcasting. The Agency must conduct the public tender procedure and make the selection on the basis of a grounded proposal by the *Broadcasting Council* and in accordance with the act regulating electronic communications (ECA).

479. In the procedure for selecting among bidders with a legitimate interest, the efficiency of *use of frequencies* and the following *criteria regarding the performance* of radio and/or television activities must primarily be taken into consideration:

- the amount of *in-house production* and production of Slovenian audio-visual works;
- the *political neutrality* of the programme service and the diversity of the programme offered in terms of genre and theme;
- the level of *development of broadcasting in the specific area* and the level of coverage achieved by the same programme service in the area under tender and the number of potential consumers (listeners or viewers) and the duration (scope) of the programme service;
- an opinion from the relevant *local community* body on the justification of covering the;

area with a new programme service and an assurance that the local community supports a local or regional radio or television programme service;
- the applicant's *economic status and technical and personnel* capacity to broadcast a radio or television programme service and the applicant's experience in broadcasting.

480. A national radio or television programme service has priority in a selection over other bidders in those *areas that it does not cover* or does not cover at a level of sufficient technical quality; priority is also e given to the special importance of radio and television. If the same or a similar range of programme is offered, in the selection of the broadcaster of a programme service that would cover a smaller area (one or several local communities or regions) priority must be given to the bidder with a head office in the area for which the programme service is intended.

IV. The Right to Disseminate Programme in Digital Broadcasting Technique

481. Article 104a of the MMA stipulates the conditions and criteria for the selection between the interested providers of the programme for obtaining the right to disseminate programme on the tendered area in *digital broadcasting technique.*

482. As for digital broadcasting technique, the Agency as well conducts the public tender procedure for the providers of the programme and makes the selection on the basis of a grounded proposal by the *Broadcasting Council* and in accordance with the Act on Audio-visual Media Services (AAMS). In agreement with the Broadcasting Council, the Agency lays down the conditions and criteria for the selection of providers for the dissemination of radio and television programme on the tendered area. In the process of selection between the interested providers of the programme in a public tender, the following must be taken into account:

- the *diversity* of the programme offered in terms of genre and theme and the proportion of in-house production;
- for a television programme, the amount of *production* of Slovenian audio-visual works and for a radio programme, the amount of Slovenian music;
- the *duration (scope) of the programme* service and adequately balanced reporting in the daily informative programme.

483. When selecting the programme service, priority must be given the programme services that are already broadcasted through analogue broadcasting radio frequencies in the tendered area and free (not encoded) programmes. The Agency decides on the submitted offers by issuing a *decision on the selection* of providers and grants the selected providers the right to disseminate their programme on the tendered area in digital broadcasting technique.

V. Radio Broadcasting Licenses

484. Every broadcaster must *acquire a radio broadcasting license* before it starts disseminating radio programming. The license is also a condition for participating in public tenders for allocating radio frequencies for broadcasting. The Agency issues a license after receiving the broadcaster's application and prior *opinion from the Broadcasting Council.*[114]

485. The conditions for acquiring a license are that the broadcaster has radio *broadcasting registered* as its activity and that a decision from the Ministry of Culture on being entered into the mass media register.

486. The application for acquiring a license *must include information* on the *radio programme broadcaster* (applicant's name, and headquarters, i.e. address, the name of the legal representative and any potential authorized person, company registration number), the *planned activity* of the broadcaster (i.e. radio broadcasting), the *name of the radio station* the broadcaster is going to broadcast and the filled out *form on basic programming requirements* which the broadcaster is following in broadcasting.

487. The procedure for acquiring the license is regulated by Articles 105 and 106 of the MMA and the General Act on Broadcasting License.

488. Article 105 of the MMA regulates licencing for performing radio or television activities; it is said that a licence for performing radio or television activities (the licence) is issued by the Agency to a broadcaster of radio or television programme service on the basis of the procedure and under *conditions set out by* MMA.

489. The applicant for the licence must dispose of with the registered radio or television activities and the decision of the competent ministry on the entry of the radio or television programme in the register of media.

490. The Agency issues an act stipulating which programme requirements the broadcaster must define in the application and the conditions under which these can be changed. A broadcaster of a radio or television programme service who obtained the licence can be granted *the right to use the radio frequencies* for disseminating its radio or television programme in *analogue technique* or the right to disseminate its radio or television programme in the tendered area in *digital technique* in accordance with MMA and ECA.

491. The licence is issued for an *unlimited period of time*. The Agency reports precise information on the issue, amendment, transfer, temporary cancellation and revocation of licences within eight days to the relevant ministry. The procedure for the issue, amendment, transfer, temporary cancellation and revocation of the decision on the licence and detailed provision on its contents is defined by the Agency.

---

114. *See*: http://www.akos-rs.si/radio-broadcasting-licenses.

492. The holder of the decision on the licence to perform a radio or television activity *may transfer the rights* arising from such licence *to another legal entity or natural person* who meets the prescribed conditions for obtaining the authorization under the condition that they do not intervene with the programme requirements from this licence. The validity of the licence is terminated if the holder is dissolved and if the programme, for which the licence had been issued, was deleted from the register of media kept by the competent ministry (MMA, Article 106).

A. *Radio Broadcasters*

1. Establishing a Radio Station

493. To establish a radio station, one must meet several requirements[115]. First it is necessary to form a *company* (public or private limited company or a partnership) and to enter radio broadcasting as the company's activity into founding act and file it with the *register of companies* at the respective The Agency of the Republic of Slovenia for Public Legal Records and Related Services (AJPES) and Commercial Court.

494. Second, it is compulsory to enter radio programme into the *mass media register* at the Ministry of Culture. Third (last but not least) it is necessary to acquire a *radio broadcasting license* from the competent Agency.

2. Broadcasting a Radio Station

495. To broadcast the radio station via radio frequencies, one must apply the station at the public *tender for the allocation of radio frequencies*, which is carried out by the Agency. For coordination of an available radio frequency and the execution of a public tender, the broadcaster needs to *file a proposal with the Agency*, in which one should list the reasons for carrying out a tender for available frequencies and technical characteristics. The proposal is only the first step in carrying out a public tender and does not by itself guarantee the acquisition of the frequency since anyone meeting the requirements can participate in the public tender.

496. To broadcast *via other platforms* (i.e. the internet), one does not need any additional licenses or rights, but to have to enter a business agreement with an individual operator.

---

115. For radio *see*: http://www.akos-rs.si/how-to-establish-a-radio-program-.

3. Obligations of Radio Programmes

497. The MMA imposes certain obligations on radio station broadcasters,[116] and the Agency monitors the implementation as part of its expert supervision. Certain legal requirements *are stricter* for RTV Slovenia's radio channels and stations of special importance.

498. Obligations of radio programmes refer to reporting on broadcasting and implementation of programming concept, further on in-house production on Slovenian music and on Radio advertising. Radio station broadcasters must submit a written *report on broadcasting* and *implementation of a programming concept* to the Agency by the end of March every year.

499. According to MMA, Article 85, *the share of in-house production must comprise at least 20%* of the daily transmission time of each television programme, of which not less than sixty (60) minutes between 18 and 22 unless otherwise specified by the law. The recurrence of a radio or television show must be clearly marked. At least 30% of the daily transmission time of each radio programme must include the content of their own production unless otherwise provided by the Act.

500. Slovenian music or music created and performed by Slovenian artists must present:

- at least 20% of all music played daily on every radio station;
- at least 40% of all music played daily on RTV Slovenia's radio stations;
- at least 25% of all music played daily on stations of special importance.

These requirements do not apply for radio stations for Hungarian and Italian minorities.

According to Article *86a (amended in 2016)*, the above shares referred to shall be achieved during the transmission time between *0 and 6 AM*, in transmission time between *6 and 18 PM* and in transmission time between the *18 and 24*. At least *70% of the share* must represent music, which is carried out in the Slovene language, except in the case of instrumental music. At least a quarter of the proportion must represent Slovenian music, which was for the first time played before two years.

501. The total share of advertisements, radio-sales, and other paid announcements on the radio programme should not exceed:

- 20% of the daily broadcasting time and 20% of each hour; or
- 15% of daily broadcasting time and 12 minutes per hour on stations of special importance.

---

116. *See*: http://www.akos-rs.si/obligations-of-radio-programs.

502. For RTV Slovenia's radio stations the total share of advertisements, radio-sales, and other paid announcements should *not exceed 15%* of daily broadcasting time, and the total share of advertisements should *not exceed 10%* of the daily broadcasting time. The share of advertisements and other paid announcements should *not exceed 12 minutes* per hour, while between 6 PM and 11 PM it should *not exceed 9 minutes* per hour. The Radio Slovenia 3 station must *not play any advertising* content. RTV Slovenia's journalists and news anchors must not appear in advertising.

4. Radio and TV Networks

503. Broadcasters of radio and TV programmes without the status of a station of special importance can also *link into regional or national networks*. A national network is a network covering *over 50%* of the population of the Republic of Slovenia. Conditions for linking into a network:[117]

- each of the linked broadcasters in the territory for which the license was issued must broadcast *at least two hours of in-house* produced programming daily;
- the total in-house production of the broadcasters linked into a network, which is broadcast in Slovenian and which excludes the programming from the previous point, amounts to *at least 25% of the programme* content broadcast on the network daily;
- each of the broadcasters linked into the network must *acquire prior approval from the Agency* if its programme concept is going to change significantly after linking into a network;
- broadcasters linked into a network prepare a *joint programming concept* and a written legal act on its implementation, and send both documents to the competent ministry for the purpose of registration in the mass media register;
- linked broadcasters *adopt a special act appointing the editor in chief* of the joint programming, who is responsible for programming broadcast, and send the act to the competent ministry 15 days before the network begins operations.

504. A radio or TV network does *not have its own license*; instead, its characteristics are entered into the licenses of individual radio stations linked into the network. A network is *not an independent station,* so it *cannot participate in public tenders* for the allocation of radio frequencies, although the stations linked into the network may participate in these tenders. Lining into Radio and TV networks is governed by Article 83 of the MMA.

117. *See*: http://www.akos-rs.si/radio-networks.

B. Television Broadcasters

1. Requirements for Television Broadcasting

505. To establish a television station, one must enter television broadcasting (60.200) as the company's activity into the *register* of companies, enter television station into the mass media register at the Ministry of Culture and acquire a television *broadcasting license* from the Agency. To disseminate *television programming via radio frequencies*, one must enter the station in the public tender for acquiring *the right to disseminate programming using digital broadcasting*, which is carried out by the Agency.

506. To disseminate *via other platforms, such as cable systems, satellites, or Intellectual Property (IP)* television, on does *not need any additional licenses* or rights, it is only necessary to conclude a business agreement with individual operators.

2. Supervising Position of the Agency

507. Under the AAMS the Agency received much *more authority and power for oversight* and enforcement, but also much greater accountability in relation to the audio-visual media sector. Numerous general acts are required by the AAMS; the regulator is responsible also for preparing the practical implementation of the AAMS. The Agency's key tasks in this area comprise providing *conditions for television* programming development and performing *expert supervision* of programming content in accordance with the MMA, and, since November 2011, also *performing inspections into programming content* and compliance with advertising rules in accordance with AVMSA,

508. The Agency's tasks are also in *protecting children* from harmful content and to make sure other rules referring to programme contents are respected.

C. Content Obligations (Quota)

1. Obligations of Television Channels

509. AVMSA transposed the AVMS Directive into Slovenian media legislation. The AVMSA brought all obligations arising from the Directive, such as rules on *identification, accessibility, incitement to hatred, protection of minors, events of major importance, short news extracts* and on the promotion of European audio-visual works, both in *linear and in on-demand* services. The latter are expected to notify their activity to the national regulator (The Agency), as the Act introduced the establishment of an official database of non-linear AVMSA providers.

510. The MMA and the AAMS obviously impose certain *obligations on television channel broadcasters*. Some obligations are stricter for the television channels of RTV Slovenia and the television channels of special importance. The obligations refer to *annual reporting, protection of children and minors, own production, Slovenian music, audio-visual works and television advertising.*

2. Reporting a Written Report

511. The issuer of media must *inform the competent ministry about any change of the data* referring to the registration of the media, within fifteen days of the creation of the change. The issuer must also give the competent ministry other information when required by them for implementing the applicable rules in the field of media (Article 14/1 of the MMA).

512. The broadcaster must send a written *report on the implementation of the activities and implementation of the programme design to the AKOS* on an annual basis by the end of the month of March (Article 14/2 of the MMA).

513. Each media registration data, with the exception of information on resources and the method of financing, and programming concepts of radio and television programmes which have not yet begun to broadcast, *is accessible to interested public* (Article 14/3 of the MMA).

3. The Share of In-House Production

514. The share of in-house production for Radio and TV is defined in detail by Article 85 of the MMA, which, among other things, states that:

- the share of in-house production must encompass *at least 20%* of daily broadcast time, of which at least 60 minutes must be between 6 PM and 10 PM;
- a *rerun of a television* show must be clearly marked; the share of own production can include only the first rerun of a program, except for reruns of television talk shows.

515. Own production is also defined in The Rules on Measures for Defining In-house Production Content. Article 85 of the MMA defines that he proportion of *in-house production* must be *at least 20%* of the daily transmission time of any *television* programme service, of which *at least sixty minutes* must be between 6 p.m. and 10 pm. Repeats of a radio or television programme must be clearly designated as such. Only the first repeat of a programme may count towards the proportion, with the exception of repeats of television discussion programmes.

516. At least *20% of the daily* transmission time of any *radio* programme service must comprise programme produced *in-house.*

4. The proportion of Slovenian Music

517. The share of *Slovenian music* is defined in detail for Radio and TV by Article 86 of the MMA, where it is stated that Slovenian music or music production from Slovenian artists and musicians should represent:

– at least 20% of all the music broadcast daily on each television channel;
– at least 40% of the music on all the television channels of RTV Slovenia;
– at least 25% of the music on all the television channels of special importance,

518. These provisions do *not apply* to television channels intended for *Hungarian and Italian minorities.*

519. According to Article 86a (amended in 2016, MMA-C), the above shares (defined in 518) shall be achieved during the transmission time between 0 and 6 AM, in transmission time between 6 and 18 PM and in transmission time between the 18 and 24. At least 70% of the above share (defined in 518) must represent music, which is carried out in the Slovene language, except in the case of instrumental music. At least a quarter of the proportion must represent Slovenian music, which was for the first time played before two years.

5. The Shares of Slovenian Audio-Visual Works

520. The Agency supervises the *shares of audio-visual works* of Slovenian producers, audio-visual works of European producers, and audio-visual works from independent European producers in the annual broadcast time.

521. Detailed requests regarding the shares of audio-visual works of Slovenian producers can be found in Articled 87 and 92 (except for paragraph 1, which is no longer applicable) of the MMA, and regarding the shares of European audio-visual works or works from independent producers in Articles 16 and 17 of the AAMS. Audio-visual works of Slovenian producers are defined also by the Regulation on the Measures and Conditions for Determining Slovenian Audio-visual Works.

522. Article 87 of the MMA defines that the *broadcaster of every television* programme service must endeavour to see that a *significant proportion* of the annual transmission time comprises Slovenian audio-visual works. Slovenian audio-visual works must account for *at least 2%* of the annual transmission time of each television programme service of a broadcaster. The broadcaster must increase the proportion of such works each year in comparison with the proportion of annual transmission time in the previous year until the proportion reaches *5% of the annual* transmission time (advertisements and telesales are not included in the annual transmission time).

6. The Proportion of European Audio-Visual Works

523. Article 16 of the AVMSA stipulates that the proportion of European audio-visual works in any television programme must account for *at least 50%* of the annual transmission time. The proportion of European audio-visual works in any *on-demand* AVMS must account for at least *10% of European* audio-visual works in the programme catalogue in any calendar year. A provider of on-demand AVMS who fails to meet the proportion of 10% must provide a *financial contribution for the production* or acquisition of rights to European audio-visual works of at least 1% of total annual revenues from its AVMS generated in a calendar year.

524. The annual transmission time does not include the time devoted to news reports, sports events, games, advertising, teleshopping and video pages.

7. The Proportion of Audio-Visual Works by Independent Producers

525. Article 17 of the AVMSA stipulates that the proportion of European audio-visual works of independent producers in any television programme must account for *at least 10%* of the annual transmission time. At least half of the works from the preceding paragraph must be produced in the last five years.

526. The annual transmission time in this article does not include the time devoted to news reports, sports events, games, and advertising, teleshopping and video pages. This restriction does not apply to local broadcasters with special interest status and television broadcasters whose programmes are intended for local audiences and are not included in the programme network reaching more than *50% of the population* of the Republic of Slovenia (restrictions do not apply to special television programmes intended for live broadcasts from the National Assembly and for television programmes intended for the autochthonous Italian or Hungarian national community).

527. The restriction also does not apply to television programmes exclusively devoted to advertising and teleshopping as well as to television programmes intended exclusively for self-promotion.

8. Reporting on Proportions

528. According to Article 18 of the AVMSA, by the end of February of each year, a broadcaster must submit to the ministry responsible for the media and to the Agency a *breakdown of the attained proportion* of European audio-visual works in the annual transmission time for the previous year. This proportion must detail the figures on the amount of the annual transmission time, data on the proportion of own production, of Slovenian audio-visual works and of audio-visual works of independent producers as well as data on the proportion of new audio-visual works. By the end of February of each year, a provider of AVMS must submit to the ministry responsible for the media and to the Agency a report on the implementation of the requirements.

529. A broadcaster who does not meet the proportion of European audio-visual works or a provider of on-demand AVMS who does not meet the requirements must submit a report to the ministry responsible for the media and to the Agency, stating the *objective reasons for its inability* to meet its legal obligations. In this event the Agency, through an inspection procedure, asks the ministry responsible for the media for an opinion on the merits of the reasons for noncompliance regarding the proportions or requirements.

530. The provisions on restrictions do not apply to local broadcasters with special interest status and broadcasters whose programmes are intended for local audiences and are not included in the programme network reaching more than 50% of the population of the Republic of Slovenia. It also does not apply to television programmes exclusively devoted to advertising and teleshopping as well as to television broadcasts intended exclusively for self-promotion.

9. Special Programme Requirements for RTV Slovenia

531. Article 92 of the MMA stipulates that *Slovenian* audio-visual works must together make up *at least 25%* of the annual transmission time of RTV Slovenia television programme services 1 and 2 and one quarter of this share must be *created by independent* producers.

532. The audio-visual works of independent producers must comprise at least *10%* of the annual transmission time of RTV Slovenia television programme services, which includes the share of Slovenian audio-visual works created by independent producers. Time devoted to advertisements, news, sports events, game shows, teletext and telesales does not count. This provision does not apply to special national television programmes.

10. Programme Concept

533. The purpose of publication and the basic substantive guidelines for the operation of a mass medium must be set out by a broadcaster through the programme concept. The programme concept of a radio or television programme service must also contain a *programme scheme, which defines* (Article 17 of the MMA):

– the type of programme, and/or classification thereof into programme areas;
– the anticipated quantitative ratio between individual programme areas;
– the anticipated maximum amount of advertising content;

– the anticipated amount of in-house production and production of Slovenian audio-visual works.

534. The broadcaster of a television programme service must also stipulate in the programme concept the initial proportions of works of European audio-visual production, European audio-visual works by independent producers and Slovenian audio-visual works. A broadcaster must obtain the editorial board's opinion prior to a fundamental change or significant addition to the programme concept. A broadcaster must obtain prior *approval from the Agency for a fundamental change* or significant addition to the programme concept of a radio or television programme service and submit the editorial board's opinion on the intended change or addition.

535. The programme concept must be a *constituent part of employment contracts* between the publisher and editorial personnel and between the publisher and journalists. The special rights of editorial personnel and journalists deriving from changes or additions to the programme concept are defined by the branch collective agreement.

536. This provision *does not apply to local, regional and student broadcasters* of television programme services if the individual programme service is intended for local inhabitants and is not included in a national network. This provision does not apply to television programme services specializing in telesales or self-promotion.

D. Language Requirements

1. Protection of the Slovene Language

537. Publishers founded and registered in the Republic of Slovenia must disseminate *programme in Slovene, or must translate* the programme into Slovene in an appropriate manner, unless such is primarily intended for readers, listeners or viewers from any other language group. Publishers may disseminate programme intended for *language education* in a foreign language. The reason for disseminating programme in a foreign language or the purpose thereof must be separately elaborated in a discernible position within/on the programme medium using clear graphic, visual or acoustic symbols in Slovene (Article 5 of the MMA).

538. If, for reasons of the immediacy, directness and authenticity of informing the public, or because of unavoidable time or technical obstacles or other unforeseen obstacles, the programme is exceptionally disseminated in *a foreign language* the opinion on the matter must be issued by the competent minister (Article 5 of the MMA).

539. The *name of the medium* and its programmes or columns must be in the Slovene language (allowed also in a dead language, Esperanto or one of the Slovene dialects; in the case of doubts the opinion is issued by the competent minister) with the exception of those media or its columns or programmes which are the Slovene licensed versions of a foreign medium or columns or programmes with trademarks or service marks of such medium (Article 5 of the MMA).

E. Representation of Minorities on the Screen

540. Slovene media legislation has comprehensive rules and principles referring to different types of minorities. For example, according to Article 2of the MMA, citizens' *right to public information* and *to be informed in general* belongs equally to the Slovene minorities in Austria, Hungary and Italy, the Hungarian and Italian ethnic communities in Slovenia, and the Romani community living in Slovenia and also to Slovenes around the world.

541. At the same time, the ARTV stipulates that RTV Slovenia covers Roma community, members of national communities of the former Yugoslav republics (Albanians, Bosnians, Montenegrins, Croats, Macedonians and Serbs), and members of other national and ethnic communities in the Republic of Slovenia.

§3. Protection of Minors

I. Protection of Children and Minors

542. *Protection of children and minors* is defined in detail in Article 14 of the AVMSA, which, among other things, defines that television channels must *not broadcast content that might seriously harm* the physical, mental, or moral development of children and minors, especially any content that contains pornography or depicts gratuitous violence. The broadcasting of potentially harmful content is *permissible, if it is limited by technical means* and a properly selected broadcast time so that children and minors have no access to it under normal conditions.

543. Content that is not suitable for *children and minors under 12* may be broadcast after 9 PM, content not suitable for children and minors *under 15* after 10 PM, and content not suitable for children and minors *under 18* after 12 AM, but such content may be broadcast until 5 AM at the latest.

544. The broadcasters of television channels are obliged to broadcast an appropriate audio and visual *warning before broadcasting* potentially harmful content, and during the broadcast this content must be marked with an appropriate visual symbol (the minister in charge of the media sets the sound and visual warning, the visual symbol, and the manner of broadcasting).

545. The protection of children and minors is also defined in *The Rules* on Assigning the Visual and Sound Warning for Content That Is Not Suitable for Children and Minors (the general act based on the AVMSA and named The Rules the Protection of Children and Minors in Television Programmes and On-Demand Audio-visual Media Services).

546. Programme content which might seriously impair the physical, mental or moral development of children and adolescents may be available by way of *on-demand* AVMS only in a manner ensuring that children and adolescents will not normally hear or see such programmes (Article 15 of the AVMSA).

II. Ethical Code on the Aesthetic and Ethical Criteria

547. The aesthetic and ethical criteria for presenting the programme, works or scenes and the showing of the appropriate warnings and symbols must be defined by the broadcaster of television programme with their *internal rules (ethical codes)* which must be available to the general public all the time.

548. The rules must also define the *possibilities of complaints* for the viewer's objecting to the implementation of the criteria. The broadcasters of television programme must send a copy of their internal rules to the competent ministry and the Broadcasting Council within 15 days of their adoption and inform the abovementioned of any changes within the same deadline.

549. Every year, the broadcasters of television programme *must submit to the competent ministry* and the Broadcasting Council *a report* on the implementation of internal rules which must include the data on received complaints of the viewers and their resolving by no later than the end of February for the previous year.

550. The competent minister passes the appropriate secondary legislation to determine the *visual symbol and the acoustic and visual warning* and the manner of presenting them, as well as stipulate a plan for their promotion.

551. Access to *pornographic contents* in electronic publications must be limited, by means of appropriate technical protection, in such a way that children and minors cannot access them.

552. The annual report prepared by the Broadcasting Council for the National Assembly must contain the assessment of the implementation of the above provisions.

§4. Human Dignity (Prohibition of Hate Speech)

553. There are a number of legal provisions related to human dignity and the prohibition of hate speech in media legislation (MMA and ARTV). For example, the provision of MMA related to *prohibition of incitement to inequality and intolerance.*

554. Article 8 of the MMA explicitly prohibits the dissemination of programme that encourages national, racial, religious, sexual or any other *inequality, or violence and war,* or incites national, racial, religious, sexual or any other *hatred and intolerance.*

Article 9 of the AVMSA imposes a *prohibition on promoting inequality and intolerance.* It is prohibited to promote national, racial, religious, sexual or other inequality, to violence and war, and to challenge national, racial, religious, sexual or other hatred and intolerance through AVMS. It is prohibited to disrespect human dignity through AVMS.

555. However, there are a number of respective provisions in the *Code* of Ethics of Slovene Journalists (Code). Code for ex. stipulates, that journalist should at all times follow the principles of reporting in an *accurate and conscientious manner.* Such conduct of journalists is the cornerstone of their credibility.

556. The journalist should, according to Code, *verify the accuracy* of information gathered and exercise care to avoid mistakes. Each mistake – however inadvertently – should, according to Code, be admitted and corrected. When publishing information involving serious allegations, the journalist should try to receive a *response from those affected.* When publishing *unconfirmed* information or speculation, this should, according to Code, be expressly pointed out by the journalist.

557. The journalist, according to Code, should respect the *individual's right to privacy* and avoid *sensationalistic and unjustified disclosure* to the public of anyone's privacy. Intrusion into an individual's privacy is only permissible if there is an overriding public interest. With public officials and others seeking power, influence and attention the public's right to be informed is greater.

558. The journalist should be aware that gathering and publishing information and photographs may *cause harm to individuals* not accustomed to media and public attention. Reporting on judicial matters, the journalist should, according to Code, take into consideration that no one is guilty until legally found so.

§5. Right of Reply

559. Issues related to right to correction and right to reply are *elaborated in PART I,* dealing with Freedom of Expression and apply entirely to broadcasting media as well.

Chapter 3. Political Broadcasting

§1. Rules on Political Independence of Broadcasters

I. Political Propaganda Is Not Permitted

560. Article 10 of the ARTV stipulates that political propaganda is not permitted on the channels of RTV Slovenia. Irrespective of this provision, political propaganda is permitted *during the period of election* campaigns in accordance with the provisions of the Act regulating election campaigns.

561. Political propaganda pursuant to ARTV is political propaganda messages (spots) and other forms of political propaganda whose purpose is to influence the stance of voters in casting their votes in elections. RTV Slovenia may only transmit *political party broadcasts* along with the name of the source commissioning the broadcast. The source commissioning the broadcast is responsible for the content of such messages.

II. Religious Promotional Messages Are Not Permitted

562. Also *religious promotional messages are not permitted* on the channels of RTV Slovenia. Religious promotional messages pursuant to ARTV are paid advertisements for religious communities (Article 11 of the ARTV).

§2. Fair Representation in Election Periods

I. Free of Charge Presentations in Election Campaigns

563. During election campaigns, RTV Slovenia has, according to Article 12 of the ARTV, to provide a portion of programme time for the *presentation of candidates, political parties* and their manifestoes *free of charge.*

564. In determining the time and formulation of the content of such broadcasts, RTV Slovenia is bound to adhere to the principle of ensuring credible and impartial informational broadcasts whereby it has to provide comprehensive information regarding political events at home and in neighbouring countries (Article 4 of the ARTV).

565. The time devoted to the presentation of candidates and political parties represented in the National Assembly and European Parliament must be *the same for all*, and equally the conditions governing their presentation as part of pre-election broadcasts must also be the same.

II. Equal Time and Conditions

566. RTV Slovenia must also *ensure equal time and conditions for their presentations* for candidates for President of the Republic. Within 15 days of the announcement of elections for President of the Republic, elections for the National Assembly, the European Parliament and local elections, RTV Slovenia must announce the method, form, extent and conditions for the presentation of candidates, political parties and their manifestoes on its channels, in daily newspapers or in some other way accessible to the public.

567. Political parties and *independent candidates* that are not represented in the National Assembly or European Parliament must have at their disposal a total of *one-third of the total time* determined by RTV Slovenia for all political parties and candidates participating in the elections.

568. RTV Slovenia must *enable presentations for these parties and candidates* within the framework of special pre-election presentations intended for them in separate slots from the broadcasts referred to in the preceding paragraph, such that each of these parties and each independent candidate shall be afforded mutually equal representation (Article 12 of the ARTV).

Chapter 4. Advertising Rules

§1. Different Forms of Commercial Communications

I. Television Advertising

569. The concept of *television advertising* and the form of audio-visual commercial messages is defined in detail by the AVMSA (Articles 19–32), while in some segments, the provisions of the MMA are still applicable.

570. One of the new aspects in the regulation of television advertising brought by AAMS is *the reduction in the amount of advertising permitted* in public service television channels. Hence, RTV Slovenia can during the day broadcast 10 minutes of advertising per hour, while between 6 pm and 11 pm only 7 minutes per hour. Unlike commercial TV broadcasters, the public service broadcaster is not allowed to interrupt feature films, news shows and cultural, arts, science or educational programmes with advertising.

571. Audio-visual commercial messages must be *clearly recognizable* and must not use technical procedures that might not allow users to consciously detect such messages. Surreptitious audio-visual commercial messages are forbidden.

572. Television advertising and telemarketing must be clearly recognizable so that they can be *distinguished from editorial content*. They must be published in special segments so that they are visibly and audibly separated from other programming.

II. The Total Scope of Television Advertising

573. The total scope of television advertising and telemarketing in a television channel must not surpass *12 minutes* of any individual hour.

574. For television channels of RTV Slovenia, the total scope of television advertising and telemarketing in a television channel must *not surpass 10 minutes* of any individual hour, and *during 6 PM and 11 PM* it must *not surpass 7 minutes* of any individual hour.

575. RTV Slovenia's television channels and stations with the status *of special importance must not interrupt* television programme units such as feature films and TV films (except for serial films, TV shows, and entertainment programming), news programmes, and programmes with a cultural, artistic, scientific, or educational nature with television advertising or telemarketing.

III. Responsibility for the Advertisement

576. Article 50 stipulates that the person that commissions an advertisement is *responsible for the veracity* and accuracy of any statements or figures therein; the responsible editor is responsible for the advertisements compliance with the MMA and with the programme concept of the mass medium.

577. The person that commissions an advertisement may not influence the programme concept and editorial independence of a mass medium.

578. Article 51 stipulates that it is *obligatory to disseminate advertisements in Slovene* or in a Slovene translation, unless disseminated in a foreign language in accordance with the AASM. Mass media for the Hungarian and Italian ethnic communities may publish advertisements in the language of the ethnic community.

IV. Audio-Visual Commercial Communications

579. Article 19 of the AVMSA sets out the issue of the visibility of audio-visual commercial communications. It is stipulated that audio-visual commercial communications must be clearly identified as such.

580. Surreptitious audio-visual commercial communication is prohibited. Audio-visual commercial communications must not use technical procedures that would prevent users from consciously recognizing such communications.

§2. Restrictions on Content

I. Prohibited Audio-Visual Commercial Communications

581. Article 20 of the AVMSA stipulates that audio-visual commercial communications must not *prejudice respect for human dignity.* Commercial communications must also not *include or promote any discrimination* based on sex, race or ethnic origin, nationality, religion or belief, disability, age or sexual orientation;

582. Commercial communications are *prohibited from encouraging behaviour* or actions prejudicial to human health or safety, environmental protection or cultural heritage.

II. Protection of Minors Regarding Audio-Visual Commercial Communications

583. Article 21 of the AVMSA stipulates that audio-visual commercial communications must not cause physical, mental or moral detriment to minors. Therefore audio-visual commercial communications *may not in particular* encourage minors to buy or hire a product or service by exploiting their inexperience or credulity and/ or to persuade their parents or others to purchase the advertised goods or services.

584. Audio-visual commercial communications *may further not* exploit the trust minors place in parents, teachers or other persons and/or unreasonably show minors in dangerous situations.

III. Prohibition of Audio-visual Commercial Communications

585. Article 22 of the AVMSA stipulates that audio-visual commercial communications for *tobacco* and tobacco products, medicinal products and alcoholic beverages are governed by *special rules*. Audio-visual commercial communications for health care activities, health services or health care service providers are prohibited, unless otherwise provided by a special law.

586. Article 23 of the AVMSA regulates audio-visual commercial communications *for foods in children's* programmes. It stipulates, that providers must develop a *code of conduct* regarding inappropriate audio-visual commercial communication, accompanying or included in children's programmes, of foods containing nutrients and substances with a nutritional or physiological effect, as, in particular those such as fat, trans fatty acids, salt/sodium and sugars, excessive intakes of which in the overall diet are not recommended (hereinafter: code of conduct), and must make it public.

587. The code of conduct must be designed in a manner to enable children the development of *healthy eating habits* in accordance with dietary guidelines published by the minister of health. Providers must submit a copy of the code of conduct to the ministry responsible for the media and to the Agency within 15 days of its adoption, and notify them of any amendment thereof within the same period.

IV. Television Advertising and Teleshopping

588. Article 27 of the AVMSA highlights the visibility and *differentiation* between television *advertising and teleshopping*. Television advertising and teleshopping must be readily *recognizable* so that they can be distinguishable from editorial content.

589. Television advertising and teleshopping may be *aired in special time slots* so that they are visually and audibly clearly separated from other programmes. Free of charge advertising must be distinctly identified as such.

V. Restrictions on Television Advertising and Teleshopping

590. Article 28 of the AVMSA sets out that television advertising and teleshopping *must not be* aired in a television programme *during individual programme* units or programmes, unless they are broadcast in such a way that the content integrity of the programme does not suffer, taking into account the nature and length of the programme and breaks in the duration of the programme intended for that purpose.

591. Television advertising and teleshopping must also not be aired in a manner that would *infringe the rights of holders of copyright* and related rights.

592. When broadcasting a programme unit or a programme, consisting of *separate, independent parts* (e.g. sporting events), the television channel may broadcast television advertising and teleshopping only between the end of one independent section and the beginning of the next or during interruptions and breaks.

593. Television advertising and teleshopping are *not allowed* during the coverage of *state or religious* ceremonies.

VI. Restrictions on Advertising to Specific Television Programmes

594. Article 29 of the AVMSA *prohibits RTV Slovenia to interrupt* television programme units, such as feature films or films made for television (excluding series, serials, series and documentaries), daily *news* programmes and programmes of a cultural, artistic, scientific or educational nature, *with television advertising* and teleshopping, regardless of the duration of an individual *programme* unit.

595. This provision *also applies to local, regional, student* and non-commercial television programmes that enjoy special interest status.

596. Article 30 of the AVMSA sets out the explicit *prohibition* of television advertising and teleshopping for *medicinal products*, which require a commercial permit under the rules governing medicinal products, as well as teleshopping for health care services.

§3. Time and Frequency Restrictions

I. Restricted Scope of Television Advertising and Teleshopping

597. Article 32 of the AVMSA prohibits that the total amount of television advertising and teleshopping *exceed 12 minutes within each hour*. The total amount of television advertising and teleshopping within a single television programme of RTV Slovenia may not exceed ten minutes within each hour and may not exceed seven minutes within each hour between 6 pm and 11 pm. Between 6 pm and 11 pm an individual television programme of RTV Slovenia is not allowed to air teleshopping windows.

598. This rules do not apply to announcements aired by the broadcaster in its own channel regarding its own programmes on that channel and to ancillary products directly derived from them (i.e., products that are specifically designed for listeners or viewers to benefit fully from these programmes or to interact with them), as well as to sponsorship messages and product placement and to teleshopping windows.

II. Special Restrictions on Journalists and News Presenters

599. According to Article 99 of the MMA, *television journalists* and *news presenters* may not appear in advertising.

600. This prohibition also applies to journalists and news presenters on RTV Slovenia radio programme services.

§4. Sponsorship

I. Requirements and Restrictions Regarding Sponsorship

601. Article 24 of the AVMSA stipulates that in the case of sponsorship of AVMS or programmes, their content and in the case of television programmes their scheduling *may not be influenced* in such a way *as to affect* the responsibility and editorial independence of the provider.

602. AVMS or programmes that are sponsored *may not directly encourage* the purchase or rental of goods or services, in particular by making special promotional references to those goods or services.

603. The *placement of products, services or trademarks* of the programme's sponsor in the sponsored programme *is not permitted*, except in cases which are, according to law, *not considered as product placement.*

604. Viewers must be clearly *informed of the existence of sponsorship* (sponsorship announcement). Sponsored programmes must be clearly identified as such by the sponsor's name, logo or any other of its symbols or distinctive signs. The sponsor's name, logo or any other of its symbols or distinctive signs must be displayed at the beginning, after any breaks and at the end of the sponsored programme.

II. No Sponsorship

605. Article 25 of the AVMSA *prohibits news and information programmes to be sponsored*, unless otherwise stipulated by the law regulating elections and referendum campaigns.

606. The sponsorship of AVMS or programmes by a natural or legal person whose activities include the manufacture or sale of *medicinal products and health* care services may promote the name or image of these perso1ns, but it is *prohibited* to promote health care services or medicinal products *available and dispensed only on prescription.*

607. Sponsorship by natural or legal persons whose activity is the manufacture or sale of tobacco and tobacco products is governed by special regulations.

§5. Product Placement

I. General Prohibition of Product Placement

608. Article 26 of the AVMSA *prohibits product placement*, except in cases defined in AVMSA. Product placement, in accordance with AVMSA, is not considered as surreptitious commercial communication.

609. Product placement is *permitted* in cinematographic works, films, feature-documentary films, in series and serials produced for AVMS, and in sports and entertainment programmes.

610. Product placement is also permitted *in cases where there is no payment* but only the provision of certain goods or services free of charge, such as production props and prizes, with a view to their inclusion in a programme. If the value of goods or services is negligible in proportion to the production costs of programmes, it is considered that no product placement has occurred.

II. Product Placement Requirements

611. Programmes that contain product placement *must meet the following requirements*:

- their content and, in the case of television broadcasting, their scheduling may in no circumstances be *influenced by product placement* in such a way as to affect the responsibility and editorial independence of the provider;
- product placement may *not directly encourage the purchase* or rental of goods or services, in particular by making special promotional references to those goods and services;

– product placement *may not give undue prominence* to goods or services and programmes containing product placement must be appropriately identified at the start and at the end of the programme, and when a programme resumes after a break, in order that the viewer is clearly informed of the fact that the programme contains product placement.

612. Product placement is *not allowed* in programmes aimed at *children.*

Chapter 5. Right to Information

§1. Short News Reporting

I. Right to Make a Short Report

613. Exclusive rights and the right to short news reports in television programmes are set out by the Article 33 of the AVMSA, saying, that *every broadcaster* established in a Member State of the EU *has the right*, on conditions that are fair, reasonable, non-discriminatory and announced in a timely manner, *to broadcast short news reports* about all significant events and other events in the public interest, exclusively transmitted by the broadcaster under the jurisdiction of the Republic of Slovenia.

614. A broadcaster established in a Member State of the EU applies to the broadcaster under the jurisdiction of the same Member State of the EU, who has acquired exclusive rights, to obtain access.

615. A short news report *means a maximum of 90 second*-long extract from the broadcaster's signal, which exclusively broadcasts the event. Extracts may be used solely for general news programmes and in a non-linear manner only if the same programme is offered on a deferred basis by the same broadcaster.

Part IV. Ownership Regulation

§1. INTRODUCTION

I. Former Socially-Owned Enterprises

616. Before the reforms in the early 90, after separation from former Yugoslavia, all companies (enterprises) including all media undertakings, were socially owned. This was not state ownership, but a sui generis non-ownership concept based upon self-management, rather than property based corporate governance.

617. Privatization of Slovenia's socially-owned enterprises (including media enterprises) in the early 1990s was effected by *allocation of shares* to a combination of public funds, employees and former employees and public sale of shares.

II. Privatization Models in Slovenia

618. Privatization law has predominantly *influenced the ownership structure of economy, including media companies;* three main models of privatization were brought about.

619. Model 1 (Privatization by Public Sale)

- a substantial part (40%) of privatized company shares were *sold to the general public* in the market;
- *mandatory free distribution* of up to 20% of shares to the *employees, ex-employees* and their relatives and after;
- *mandatory allocation of 40%* to the *three funds* (Development – 20%, Indemnity – 10% and Pension Funds – 10%), which caused most of the widely diffused ownership structure.

620. Model 2 (Internal Buy Out)

- a *substantial part (40%)* of privatized shares were *sold to the employees, with five-year deferred payment* terms, possibly out of the corporation's *profits*;
- the mandatory *free distribution of up to 20% of shares to the employees,* ex-employees and their relatives;

- allocating a *compulsory 40% to the three funds* (Development – 20%, Indemnity – 10% and Pension Funds – 10%) which created the majority (up to 60%) of the internal diffused ownership structure.

621. Model 3 (Management or Other Buy Outs)

- a *substantial part (40%)* of privatized shares were sold to a *group of managers*, or a *corporation formed for that specific purpose* (usually called a *by-pass corporation because* it normally continued the business after the *privatized corporation went bankrupt*);
- *mandatory free distribution of up to 20%* of shares to the *employees, ex-employees* and their relatives; and
- a *compulsory 40% to the three funds* (Development – 20%, Indemnity – 10% and Pension Funds – 10%), which normally led to a *closed corporation* in the sense of *firm control of the privatized corporation* by the acquiring corporation or group.

622. As a result, Slovene corporate share ownership was than bifurcated between large, potentially influential i*nstitutiona*l shareholders and diffused, relatively powerless, small holders.

III. State's Ownership Control

623. Many industrial branches are still under state's control. The following industrial branches are under direct or at least indirect (as subsidiaries) ownership control of the state: broadcasting (national radio and TV), energy (all electricity production, transfer and distribution including, water and heating, nuclear and other power and mines, transport, post and telecommunications, some of the steel, iron and aluminium industries, major banks and investment companies.

624. Public (state and municipal) ownership is notwithstanding this the result of the privatization process, *still very widespread in the vital sectors of the economy and society.*

IV. Ownership Paradox in Slovenia

625. The privatization of the economy (more correctly: the transformation from social to state and private forms of enterprises) caused the *strengthening of the public sector.* The State as an owner thereby took over total *public services including national broadcasting* and, in addition, became the owner of substantial parts of *other businesses. State and parastatal institutions* (funds, investment companies, public banks) *today own more than 50% of the economy in Slovenia.*

V. Protection of Media Plurality and Diversity

626. Section 9 of the MMA deals with the issues on protection of media plurality and diversity; it regulates issues like *restriction of ownership* and *concentrations, connected persons* and issues related to *incompatibility of performing* radio and television activities.

§2. Ownership Restrictions

I. Restriction of Cross-Ownership of Printed and Broadcasting Media

627. Article 56 of the MMA sets out restriction of cross-ownership. It refers to *publisher of a daily* informative *printed medium* or a *single legal or natural person* or group of *connected persons* and to o a broadcaster of a radio or television programme service.

628. If the mentioned persons hold an ownership stake (or management or voting rights) of more than 20%, such persons may not also be the publisher or a co-founder of the broadcasting media; meaning, it may not also be broadcaster of a radio or television programme service and may not perform radio or television activities.

629. There is also vice versa restriction: it refers to a *broadcaster* of a radio or television programme service or a single legal or natural person or group of connected persons. If these persons hold an ownership stake (or a share in the management or voting rights) of more than *20%* they may *not also be the publisher* or a co-founder of the publisher of a daily informative *printed medium.*

II. General Ownership Restriction

630. There is also a *general prohibition* for those, who already own a *20% and more* of some media company.

631. Namely a publisher/broadcaster, a legal or natural person or a group of connected persons may hold an ownership stake (or management or voting rights) of *no more than 20%* of any other publisher/broadcaster.

III. Connected Persons

632. For the purpose of ownership restrictions, there is the definition of connected persons in the MMA. Under the *Article 57* of the MMA connected persons are *persons that are connected* in terms of *management or capital* or are otherwise connected because they *jointly formulate business policy or operate* in a coordinated manner with the *intent of attaining joint objectives.* Connected are also such persons that one person has the opportunity to direct any other person or significantly influence the person in making decisions on financing and operations or in deciding on the programme concept of a mass medium.

633. By MMA, for example, are *deemed connected persons* those related by blood as close family members (parents, children, siblings, adoptive parents and adopted children), married persons or persons in a non-marital union, those related through marriage/non-marital union as close family members of a spouse or non-married partner.

634. In addition *connected persons are for example deemed* such that one person or, together, persons deemed to be connected according to the other points hold(s) a commercial stake, shares or other rights on the basis of which the person(s) participate(s) in the management of another person with *at least 20%* of the voting rights.

§3. Restriction of Concentration

I. Approval for 20% or More

635. Restriction of concentration is set out in the Article 58 of the MMA for a broadcaster of a radio or television programme service or a publisher of general informative printed journal.

636. MMA stipulates that *a*ny person who wishes to acquire an ownership or management stake or a share in the voting rights in the assets of a broadcaster or a publisher *of 20% or more* is obliged *to obtain approval* from the relevant ministry for the conclusion of the legal transaction to be valid.

637. All legal transactions or resolutions of the General Meeting or another competent body of a company that are not approved are *deemed null and void.*

II. Monopoly or Prevailing Position

638. The competent ministry may refuse to issue approval to any person:

(1) which would, by means of acquiring an ownership or management stake or a share in the voting rights obtain *monopoly on the advertising* market by itself or together with a group of associated persons:
(2) which would *establish a prevailing position* in the media sphere by achieving, itself or together with a group of associated persons, the coverage of *more than 15%* of the Republic of Slovenia:
   – with analogue low-lying terrestrial radio programmes,

– with regard to the overall coverage of this area by all radio programme services diffused through analogue low-lying terrestrial radio technique over the radio frequencies for analogue broadcasting.

III. Refuse to Issue Approval

639. Refuse to issue approval is also possible to any person, which would establish a prevailing position in the media sphere by achieving, itself or together with a group of associated persons, the coverage of *more than 30%* of the Republic of Slovenia with analogue low-lying terrestrial *television programmes*, with regard to the overall coverage of this area by all television programme services diffused through analogue low-lying terrestrial radio technique over the radio frequencies for analogue broadcasting

640. Refuse is also possible if the person would achieve, itself or together with a group of associated persons, a prevailing market share with the number of the issued copies of the journals *exceeding 40%* of all sold copies of general informative *printed journals* in the Republic of Slovenia issued at least three times a week (Article 58 of the MMA).

§4. Incompatibility of Performing Radio and Television Activities

I. Incompatibility of Performing Advertising and Radio and Television Activities

641. Performing advertising and radio and television activities is incompatible. An *advertising organization may not be the broadcaster* or the founder of a broadcaster. Article 60 of the MMA refers to an *advertising organization* whose activity is the collection, design and dissemination of advertisements, and to legal or natural person or group of connected persons that hold(s) an ownership stake of *more than 10%* or a share of the voting or management rights of *more than 10%* in the capital or assets of such an organization.

642. Such an organization *may not be at the same time the broadcaster* or the founder of a broadcaster of a radio or television programme service, and may not hold a stake of *more than 20%* in the capital or a share of more than 20% of the management or voting rights in the assets of a broadcaster of a radio or television programme service.

II. Incompatibility of Performing Telecommunications Activities and Radio and Television

643. Also *operator that provides telecommunications* services may *not be the broadcaster*. Incompatibility of performing telecommunications activities and radio and television activities is regulated by Article 61 of the MMA.

644. It is said that an operator that provides telecommunications services may *not be the broadcaster* of a radio or television programme service, and may not disseminate programme or advertising, unless the licence for performing radio or television activities is obtained.

III. Protection of Competition

645. The regulations on protection of competition apply to broadcasters of mass media and operators.

646. The relevant ministry participates in the procedures of the body responsible for protection of competition relating to the concentration of publishers/broadcasters of mass media and operators; the Agency also participates in those procedures relating to broadcasters of radio and television programme services (Article 62 of the MMA).

IV. Criticism on Media Ownership in Slovenia

647. According to Human Rights Press Point[118] *the media ownership situation* is result of the *specific model of privatization* implemented after the break of socialism in early 1990s. The model enabled the state to keep significant portion of ownership in privatized companies through state-controlled funds. In past 15 years the media privatized according to that model, especially national daily newspapers, have been subject of constant trade with ownership shares mostly on the basis of political interests and under influence of political parties in power.

648. At the same time *the public service broadcasting* has never finished transformation from state-controlled broadcasting, being, especially on the basis of last regulation (from 2005), easy target of control and influence of the political groups in power.

649. Also the distribution of advertisements of the state-controlled companies have been used *by political groups* in power, most obviously in the period of the actual government, to support loyal and penalize critical media.

118. Human Rights Press Point: http://www.humanrightspoint.si/node/7.

650. The main press agency *STA is completely owned by the government*; the actual government appointed for general manager of the agency in 2007 an advisor in the prime minister's cabinet, whose appointment was followed by the change of the chief editor and editorial policy.

651. According to Human Rights Media Watch, from 2009, cases of *media freedom violations* in Slovenia were generated in that period by the media ownership situation, and by the role of the state in the media sector. It is also a consequence of the established relations between the media and the politics.[119]

US Department of State in 2016 Report for Slovenia[120] stated that reports of *political pressures on the media continued*. There were *no reported prosecutions of hate speech* during the year. A change in interpretation of regulations to identify the internet as a public space allows police to levy fines for online hate speech, although there were no reports that authorities exercised this authority. The Slovenian Association of Journalists and media analysts observed that *standards of journalistic integrity suffered because of economic pressure*; non-standard forms of employment, such as freelance or student status; and reduced protections for journalists, leading some to practice self-censorship in order to maintain steady employment. Journalists noted efforts to investigate and publish stories about local corruption cases were particularly challenging because of economic and political pressure. Private radio station owners were *critical of the changes in law that require majority of the Slovenian music* quota to be filled during daytime hours, with a quarter of it dedicated to music that is less than two years old. The government *did not restrict or disrupt access to the internet* or censor online content, and there were no credible reports that the government monitored private online communications without appropriate legal authority. According to the data from the International Telecommunication Union, *73 % of individuals in the country used the internet in 2015.* In the first quarter of 2017, 79% of persons aged 16–74 years used the internet (regular internet users) (75% in 2016); 68% used the internet every day or almost every day (64% in 2016); 18% of persons aged 16–74 years never used the internet.[121]

---

119. *Ibid.*
120. US Department of State, Bureau of Democracy, Human Rights and Labour, Country Reports on Human Rights Practices for 2016 Freedom of Speech and Press also points out the following case: In March an opposition Member of Parliament sent a series of tweets implying that two TV Slovenia journalists were prostitutes and the public broadcaster a brothel. Parliament debated the incident, and in response to defamation suits filed by the journalists, courts found the tweets to be defamatory and awarded the journalists 6,000 euros ($6,600) each in damages.
121. Republic of Slovenia, Statistical office: https://www.stat.si/StatWeb/en/News/Index/6998.

§5. Restrictions of Board Member Positions (Conflict of Interest)

I. The Broadcasting Council

652. Broadcasting council is, according to the law, politically *independent expert* body, responsible for the most important decisions in the field of broadcasting and for drawing up an annual report or assessment of the situation in the area of broadcasting and proposals for improving the situation for the National Assembly.

653. The Broadcasting Council *consists of seven members*, who are appointed by the National Assembly on the basis of a public invitation. Candidates – experts in the field of law, telecommunications and information science, audio-visual culture, economy, journalism and communicology can respond to the public invitation.

654. According to Article 101 of the MMA, the following *may not be members* of the Broadcasting Council:

- officials, parliamentary deputies and other persons employed in state bodies;
- members of the leadership of political parties;
- persons employed at a broadcaster of a radio or television programme service or at an advertising organization;
- persons who as external contractors have concluded contractual relations with the broadcaster of a radio or television programme service or an advertising organization.

655. The members of Broadcasting Council may also not be the persons *who hold more than 1%* of the capital or management or voting rights within the assets of a broadcaster of a radio or television programme service or within an advertising organization.

II. Members of the ECC of the RS

656. According to Article 229 of the ECA, members of the ECC of the RS should be neutral, disinterested and free of any conflict of interest. They may *not be members of bodies of political parties*, officers under the act governing the public sector pay system and public officials in state bodies.

657. Council members may *not be persons employed by an operator*, members of the *supervisory or management board* of an organization that performs activities subject to regulation that falls within the competence of the Agency, or persons holding ownership stakes in organizations engaged in activities subject to direct regulation that falls within the competence of the Agency or in organizations with ownership stakes in such organizations.

658. Council members may also *not be persons whose spouse*, extra-marital *partner* or civil partner under the act governing same-sex partnerships or direct *relation* up to and including the *second degree* serves as a member of the management or supervisory board of an organization that performs a business activity in an area which the Agency is competent to regulate. Council members may also *not be persons* who have ownership stakes in an organization that performs a business activity in an area which the Agency is competent to regulate or in an organization which has an ownership stake in such an organization.

III. The AKOS Council

659. Article 176 of the ECA defines incompatibility of the members of the Agency Council. Members of the Agency Council *may not be members of bodies of political parties, officers* under the act governing the public sector pay system and public officials in state bodies.

660. Members of the Agency Council may also *not be persons who are employed* by or who serve as members of the management or supervisory board of legal entities that perform an activity in an area which the Agency is competent to regulate, or who have ownership stakes in legal entities that perform an activity in an area which the Agency is competent to regulate or in legal entities which have an ownership stake in such legal entities;

661. Members of the Agency Council may also not be *person whose spouse, extra-marital partner or civil partner* under the act governing same-sex partnerships or direct relation up to and including the second degree serves as a member of the management or supervisory board of a legal entity that performs a business activity in an area which the Agency is competent to regulate, or who has ownership stakes in legal entities that perform an activity in an area which the Agency is competent to regulate or in legal entities which have an ownership stake in such legal entities.

IV. The Director of the Agency

662. The director and his deputies, their spouses, extra-marital partners, partners under the act governing same-sex partnerships or direct relations up to and including the second degree may not (*incompatibility* under Article 183 of the ECA):

- perform activities themselves as natural persons in an area which the Agency is competent to regulate;
- be members of the management or administrative body of a legal entity that performs an activity in an area which the Agency is competent to regulate;

– have ownership stakes in legal entities that performs an activity in an area which the Agency is competent to regulate or in legal entities which have an ownership stake in such legal entities.

Amended ECA in Article 183.a (*business restriction*) stipulates that the director and his deputies shall not cooperate, as a natural person, in business with natural or legal persons engaged in an activity in the field governed by the agency. The director and his deputies may not be members of the administrative or supervisory body of a legal person who works in business with natural or legal persons engaged in an activity in the field governed by the agency. They may also not have equities in legal persons who engage in business with natural or legal persons engaged in an activity in the field governed by the agency, or in legal entities having a holding in such legal persons. The prohibited business cooperation referred to in the preceding paragraph does not include business cooperation due to the use of publicly available services provided by natural or legal persons engaged in an activity in the field governed by the agency.

Amended ECA in Article 183. B *(statement of interest and links of the candidate for the director)* binds the candidate for the director to make a statement revealing his interests and links held as an individual entrepreneur, or the holder of a share in the company or a member of the administrative and supervisory bodies of the companies, performing activity in the field governed by the agency, or companies, which are their suppliers of electronic communications equipment. The candidate must disclose, in particular, information on the status of the individual proprietor, the ownership interests in the companies and the membership of the administrative and supervisory bodies of those companies. The candidate must also disclose any other circumstances, which might affect the objective and impartial performance of his or her tasks. The Director must forward the declaration within thirty days of its appointment to the agency which publishes it on its website.

V. Members of the Programme Board and Supervisory Board of RTV

663. Article 20 of the ARTV stipulates that members of the Programme Board and Supervisory Board *may not cooperate commercially* with the RTV Slovenia public institution. No one can be a member of the Programming Council and the Supervisory Board at the same time.

664. During the term of office of members of the Programme Board and Supervisory Board, RTV Slovenia may employ or make cooperation contracts with their close family members, but the Programme Board and Supervisory Board *must be acquainted in advance* with such contract or employment and the reasons for such a decision.

665. Close *family members are the spouse* or person with whom he or she lives in an unmarried relationship or a registered same-sex partner relationship, children or adopted children and grandchildren and parents or adoptive parents, and other persons who live in the same household.

666. No person may be a member of the *Programme* Board and the *Supervisory* Board at the same time.

Part V. Supervision

§1. Supervision of the Implementation of the MMA

667. Administrative and inspection supervision of the implementation of the MMA is conducted by the *ministry responsible for culture* (Article 108 of the MMA).

§2. Supervision of the Implementation of Programme Requirements and Restrictions

668. Expert supervision of the implementation of the provisions of the present Act is conducted by the Agency (Article 109 of the MMA).

669. Within the framework of *expert supervision,* the Agency:

- supervises the implementation of the *programme requirements* and restrictions that apply to radio and television programme services under the MMA (Section 5 of Title II);
- supervises the implementation of the legal provisions on *special radio and television* programme services (Section 3 of Title II);
- supervises the implementation of the programme requirements to be taken into account by the broadcaster in *disseminating its programme service* (the third and the fourth indent of the first paragraph of Article 106);
- propose to the relevant ministry a *development strategy* for radio and television programme services in the Republic of Slovenia.

§3. Supervisory Competence of the Agency

670. Article 221 of the ECA regulates supervisory competence) of the Agency. The Agency oversees the *implementation of the provisions of ECA*, of the sub laws, except in cases that lie within the competence of the Information Commissioner.

671. The Agency also oversees the implementation of all *individual acts and/or measures* which it adopts pursuant to ECA.

672. The Agency also oversees implementation of the provisions *of EU regulations* in the territory of the Republic of Slovenia in the area of electronic communications which have a direct effect on the legislation of the Republic of Slovenia and which at the same time lay down supervision of their implementation by national regulatory authorities in the area of electronic communications, as well the imposition of sanctions at the level of Member States.

673. Article 222 of the ECA regulates cooperation between supervisory authorities. The Agency and the Information Commissioner *must keep each other informed* of the supervisory measures carried out, provide each other with the information necessary for carrying out supervision, and cooperate in a professional capacity.

674. In the supervisory procedure under ECA, the provisions of the *act governing inspection* and supervision are applied, unless this Act determines otherwise. If supervision is conducted by the Information Commissioner, the provisions of the act governing personal data protection have also to be applied in the supervisory procedure (Article 223 of the ECA).

675. The Agency and the Information Commissioner decide on the sanctions for violations of ECA and of the regulations issued pursuant thereto *as the offence authorities* under the act governing offences, with each responsible for their own area of supervision. The offence procedures must be resolved by the fast-track procedure in accordance with the act governing offences.

§4. Supervision of the DBA

676. Article 37 of the *DBA*[122]regulate supervision and investigative authority over violations. It stipulates that the Agency also supervises the implementation of the provisions of the DBA and regulations and general acts issued on the basis of the DBA in compliance with the act regulating inspections and the act regulating electronic communications.

677. The Agency, according to DBA, decides on violations of the DBA and regulations thereof, acting *as investigative authority* over violations in compliance with the act governing violations.

§5. Sanctioning Powers of the Agency

678. The Agency issues a *written warning to the broadcaster* and orders the elimination of the violation it determines within a period which may not be shorter than one month or longer than six months, if it determines a broadcaster of a radio

122. Digital Broadcasting Act 22 (Official Gazette of RS, no. 102/07 dated 9 11 2007, DBA, Slov.: Zakon o digitalni radiodifuziji: http://www.dzrs.si/wps/portal/Home/deloDZ/zakonodaja/izbranZakonAkt?uid=FA7DD54E1298CFFAC12577D200316115&db=urad_prec_bes&mandat=VI

or television programme service is infringing the provisions of the MMA or does not fulfil the programme requirements stated in the licence to perform the activities. The deadline may be extended for a maximum period of three months.

679. The Agency may *suspend a licence* for performing activities for a maximum of three months if it is found that the established violations have not been eliminated; it can revoke a licence for performing activities if it is found that the broadcaster, despite receiving the suspension fails to bring the broadcaster's activities into compliance with the Agency's requirements within 30 days of recommencing broadcasting.

680. *No appeal is permitted* against a ruling. An administrative dispute is possible. If during the conduct of expert supervision, the Agency discovers an infringement it is obliged to forward a proposal for initiating the infringements procedure in cases of suspicion of an infringement.

681. If the Agency determines that a programme service from abroad is being disseminated in the Republic of Slovenia in contravention of the MMA or any international treaty by which the Republic of Slovenia is bound, it must immediately *notify the responsible ministry* of such. The Agency adopts a general act to define the methodology of such expert supervision, by means of which it lays down, in detail, the method of establishing compliance with the programme requirements and limitations.

682. The broadcasters of radio or television programmes *must keep the recordings* for each day of the broadcasted programme, together with all programme and non-programme contents as broadcast subsequently within 24 hours, for at least 30 days. In the event of technical failure that caused the termination of recording, the broadcaster must immediately inform the Agency thereof.

683. *The Agency may also impose a fine for violations of the DBA* and regulations thereof in an amount higher than that indicated as the minimum for a specific violation.

§6. Administrative Supervision and Inspection of the Implementation of the AVMS

684. Article 39 of the *AVMSA*[123] regulates administrative supervision and inspection of the implementation of the AVMS, carried out by the Agency. The authorized person of the Agency, as provided by the law governing electronic communications (ECA), has the right and duty to do the following in the event of violation of the provisions of the AVMS:

123. Act on Audio-visual Media Services (Official Gazette no. 87/2011 of 19 Oct. 2011, AVMS, Slov.: Zakon o avdiovizualnih medijskih storitvah, ZAMS).

- order *measures to remedy* the irregularities and deficiencies in a manner and within the deadline set by himself;
- carry out procedures in accordance with the *law on misdemeanours*;
- report a *crime* or a criminal complaint about an offense that is punishable by law;
- propose to a *competent authority* to take action.

685. The Agency may, in case of violations of the provisions of the AVMS, in the framework of inspection *suspend the permit* of the broadcaster *or revoke the permit* of the broadcaster.

686. In cases where a provider who does not fall under the jurisdiction of the Republic of Slovenia or under the jurisdiction of another EU Member States or party to the European Convention on Trans frontier Television of the Council of Europe, broadcasts programmes which clearly seriously or grossly *violate the protection of children* and adolescents, the Agency acts as provided by the AVMS and in accordance with applicable law in the Republic of Slovenia.

687. Where such a provider by disseminating programmes promotes national, racial, religious, sexual or other inequality, violence and war, and incites to ethnic, racial, religious, sexual or other hatred and intolerance or otherwise clearly seriously or grossly violates the law of the Republic of Slovenia, the authorized person of the Agency *impose on the operator above described measures.*

688. The provisions of the *law governing inspection* apply to the procedure of supervision, unless otherwise provided by the AVMS.

§7. Monitoring of the Work of the Agency

689. Article 190 of the ECA regulates the monitoring of the work of the Agency). The *government approves the statute of the Agency* and the Agency's *programme* of work and financial plan after receiving a positive opinion from the Agency Council.

690. The Agency must keep *separate accounting records* by area of regulation, in accordance with the act governing accounting and with the regulations issued pursuant thereto. The Agency's accounts and financial reports must be inspected by a qualified auditor.

§8. Supervisory Board of RTV Slovenia

691. According to Article 26 of the ARTV, RTV Slovenia has a Supervisory Board of eleven members. The *National Assembly appoints* five members, whereby it must take into account the relative representation of political parties in the

National Assembly, four members are appointed by the government, and employees of the RTV Slovenia public institution elects two members from among themselves in a direct ballot.

692. The Supervisory Board (Article 27) has the power to *adopt the statute* on the basis of prior consent of the Programme Board, adopt the financial plan and annual report of the public institution and decide on the use of possible surplus income over expenditure and determine the price of services that are not a part of public service.

693. The Supervisory Board *determines the method of registration* and temporary or permanent de-registration of the broadcast receiving sets, determine in detail the method of paying contributions for sets and the criteria for a write-off, partial write-off, postponement and payment in instalments in accordance with ARTV.

694. The Supervisory Board *decides on tariffs and other conditions* for transmitting programmes of other broadcasters, oversee the operations of RTV Slovenia, oversee the management of accounts books and the legality of operations, and review periodical accounts.

695. The Supervisory Board *has the right to examine* all documentation of the public institution, including documentation relating to the operation of transmitters and communications, adopt its rules of procedure and organize its work, and appoints its committees in accordance with these rules of procedure.

Selected Bibliography

Adnative, 2012, Media Represented Vecer Slovenia, [ONLINE] Available at: http://www.adnative.net/germany/represented-media/factsheet/?PARAM1=VM6VM1 [Accessed 16 August 2012]

Alexander, Larry, Is There a Right of Freedom of Expression?, Cambridge University Press, 2005

Analysis of the Law on Radio and Television of the Republic of Slovenia (RTV Slovenia) by Sigve Gramstad and Eve Salomon, 2005

Annual Report of the Listener and Viewer Ombudsman (PDF), 27 October 2009.

Barendt, E. M., Freedom of the press, Farnham; Burlington: Ashgate, cop. 2009 – PF

Bašić Hrvatin, Sandra, Lenart J. Kučić: 'Slovenia'. In: Sandra Bašić Hrvatin, Lenart J. Kučić and Brankica Petković (ur.): Media Ownership and Its Impact on Media Independence and Pluralism in Slovenia and Other Post-Socialist European Countries. Ljubljana: Peace Institute, 2004, pp. 49–92.

Bervar, Gojko: 'Freedom of Non-accountability'. Ljubljana: Peace Institute, 2004

Büscher, Wolfgang; Dittmer, Stefan; Schiwy, Peter, Gewerblicher Rechtsschutz, Urheberrecht, Medienrecht: Kommentar, Köln; München: C. Heymann, 2008

Calvert, Clay, and Robert D. Richards. 2002. 'A Pyrrhic Press Victory: Why Holding Richard Jewell as a Public Figure Is Wrong and Harms Journalism.' The Loyola of Los Angeles Entertainment Law Review (April 2).

Carey, Peter, Media law, London: Sweet & Maxwell, Thomson Reuters, 2010 – PF – prosto!

Castendyk, Oliver, Dommering, Egbert, Scheuer, Alexander, Böttcher Austin, Kathrin, European media law, Wolters Kluwer; Alphen aan den Rijn: Kluwer Law International, cop. 2008. – XLV, 1379 str.: graf. prikazi; 25 cm

Clayton, Richard, Tomlinson, Hugh, Privacy and Freedom of Expression, Cambridge University Press, 2005

Crook, Tim, Comparative media law and ethics, London; New York: Routledge, 2010 – PF

Cuhalev, Jure 'Slovenian government is trying to censor the internet', published 14 Jan 2010 [ONLINE] Available at:http://www.jurecuhalev.com/blog/2010/01/14/slovenian-government-is-trying-to-censure-the-internet/ [Accessed: 17 August 2012]

Delo-Slovenia, 'Censorship in Slovenia', published Friday 11 January 2008 [ONLINE] available at:http://www.eurotopics.net/en/home/presseschau/archiv/article/ARTICLE23686 Censorship-in-Slovenia[Accessed 16 August 2012]

Selected Bibliography

European Journalist Centre. 2010. Media landscape: Slovenia. [ONLINE] Available at:http://www.ejc.net/media_landscape/article/slovenia/. [Accessed 02 August 12].

Einspieler, V., Lampe, R. et al., Medijsko pravo, Planet GV, Ljubljana 2009; – FDV

Fechner, Frank, Entscheidungen zum Medienrecht: Auswahl für Studium und Praxis, Tübingen: Mohr Siebeck, cop. 2010

Fechner, Frank, Medienrecht: Lehrbuch des gesamten Medienrechts unter besonderer Berücksichtigung von Presse, Rundfunk und Multimedia, Tübingen: Mohr Siebeck, 2011 – PF

Fechner, Frank, Fälle und Lösungen zum Medienrecht, Tübingen: Mohr Siebeck, cop. 2009 – PF

Fink, Udo; Cole, Mark D.; Keber, Tobias O., Europäisches und internationales Medienrecht, Heidelberg: C. F. Müller, cop. 2008; – PF

Gibbons, Thomas, Free speech in the new media, Farnham; Burlington: Ashgate, cop. 2009 – PF

Goldberg, David; Sutter, Gavin; Walden, Ian; Media law and practice, Oxford University Press, 2009; PF

Jones, Nora. 2003. 'Defamation Lawsuit Sparks a "Public Figure" Debate.' Rochester (N.Y.) Daily Record (May 30)

Iosifidis, Petros: 'Digital Convergence: Challenges for European Regulation', Javnost/The Public 9 (2002), 3, pp. 27–48

Keller, Perry, European and International media law: liberal democracy, trade and the new media, New York: Oxford University Press, 2011 – Univerzitetna knjižnica MB

Lester, Anthony, Freedom of Expression, v: Macdonald R. St. J. et al. (ur.), The European System for the Protection of Human Rights, Kluwer Rights, Kluwer Academic Publishers, Netherlands 1993

Media Law Institute. 2012. Media Ownership and Privatisation in Central and Eastern Europe, [ONLINE] Available at: http://www.medialaw.kiev.ua/en/Analytics/analytics/324/. [Accessed 09 August 12]

Media Policy: What Is That? AIM Press, 28 Dec. 1999. Available from www.aimpress.org.

Mekina, Igor. 'Traps of a Small Market' AIM Press. 2001. Available from www.aimpress.org.

Milosavljević Marko, Igor Vobič, Media Landscapes, Slovenia, http://ejc.net/media_landscapes/slovenia

Milosavljević, Marko, and Bašić-Hrvatin, Sandra. Who will control the controllers?. In: Lees, Tim (ed.), Ralph, Sue (ed.), Brown, Jo Langham (ed.). Is regulation still an option in a digital universe?, (Current Debates in Broadcasting, No. 9). Luton: University of Luton Press, 2000, pp. 253–257

Milosavljević, Marko. Can technical needs dictate cultural and public interests?: public service programming and the digital age in Slovenia. In: SÜKÖSD, Miklós (ed.). Public service television in the digital age: strategies and opportunities in five South-East European countries. Sarajevo: Mediacentar, 2008, pp. 39–97

Milosavljević, Marko. Medien in Slowenien. In: Huber, Silvia (ed.). Medien in den neuen EU-Staaten Mittel- und Osteuropas: inklusive Beitrittskandidat Türkei,

(Schriftenreihe Telekommunikaton, Information und Medien, Band 19). [Krems a. d. Donau]: [Donau-Universität Krems], 2006, pp. 131–150

Milosavljević, Marko. The consequences of the digital broadcasting for content production. Medijska istraž., 2009,.No. 1, pp. 43–59

Močnik, Rastko and Brankica Petković. 'Country Reports on Media', Education and Media in Southeast Europe. 9 May 2000.

Mowbay, Alastair, Cases and Materials on the European Convention on Human Rights, Butterworths, 2001

Packard, Ashley, Digital media law, Malden; Oxford; Chichester: Wiley-Blackwell, 2010 – PF

Paschke, Marian; Berlit, Wolfgang; Meyer, Claus, Hamburger Kommentar Gesamtes Medienrecht, Baden-Baden: Nomos, 2008; – PF

Piano Media, 2012. Piano Media Expands into Slovenia [ONLINE] Available at:h ttp://www.pianomedia.eu/23/piano-media-expands-into-slovenia [Accessed 9 August 2012]

Poler Kovačič, Melita: 'Ethics and Professionalization of Slovene Journalism'. Javnost/The Public 3(1996), 4, pp. 107–121

Petković, Brankica Minorities and the Media in Slovenia [This paper was originally published as a chapter in the book Media and Minorities in South East Europe, edited by Thomas A. Bauer, Vienna: South East Europe Media Organisation, 2006, pp. 675–694. http://rci.mirovni-institut.si/Docs/Brankica_Petkovic.pdf

'Regulating Digital TV in the Slovenian Media Market Frame', Agency for Post Services and Electronic Communications of the Republic of Slovenia, 2008. This part of the text is written mostly on the basis of respective APEK document.

Radio Televizija Slovenija, 2001. Basic Facts and Figures: Program and Audience Data [ONLINE] Available at: http://www.rtvslo.si/files/RTV_Slovenija/basic_fac ts.swf [Accessed 14 August 2012]

'*Share of all viewers* from 07:00 to 24:00', Media Services AGB Research on 2005, Ljubljana, 2005

Splichal, Slavko: 'Media Beyond Socialism: Theory and Practice in East-Central Europe'. Oxford: Westview Press, 1994

Statut novinarjev Slovenije – Slovenian Association of Journalists, 2006. 8 October 2009

Statut Združenja novinarjev in publicistov – Association of Journalists and Publicists. 8 October 2009

Survey and Case Study of Atypical Work in the Media Industry, International Federation of Journalists, 2006

Vobič, Igor: Newsroom Convergence in Slovenia: Newswork Environments of the Media organizations Delo and Žurnal Media, Medijska istraživanja 15 (2009), 1, pp. 5–26. 7 October 2009.

Wandtke, Artur-Axel; Bullinger, Winfried; Welser, Marcus vonFallsammlung zum Urheber- und Medienrecht: für Studium, Fachanwaltsausbildung und Praxis, München: C. H. Beck, 2010. – PF

Selected Bibliography

Index

The numbers here refer to paragraph numbers.

Made in the USA
Monee, IL
18 October 2026

66041409R10103